GOLF
—right from
the start

In the same series

BIRD WATCHING *by* Peter Clarke
COARSE FISHING *by* Alan Wrangles
DINGHY SAILING *by* Peter Copley
FLOWER ARRANGING *by* Julia Clements

G O L F
—right from the start

BY
MAX FAULKNER

with action photographs
and drawings by
GEORGE HOUGHTON

NEWNES: LONDON

First published 1965

MADE AND PRINTED IN GREAT BRITAIN BY
MORRISON AND GIBB LIMITED, LONDON AND EDINBURGH
FOR GEORGE NEWNES LTD., TOWER HOUSE, SOUTHAMPTON
STREET, LONDON, W.C.2

CONTENTS

	About The Author	vii
	Foreword by George Houghton	ix
	This Glorious Game!	xi
1	Making A Start—The Arc	13
2	How to Hold The Club and 'Feel'	17
3	Setting Yourself Up—The Stance	20
4	Winding Up The Backswing	24
5	Swinging Down and Following Through	30
6	Timing—The Great Secret	33
7	Choosing Clubs	37
8	How to Hit The Long 'Uns!	41
9	Now For The Irons	46
10	Near The Green—How to Play Match-winners	49
11	Putting—A Game within A Game	53
12	Recovering From Sand	60
13	Coping with Natural Hazards	64
14	Bogeys, Birdies, and Forms of Play	68
15	Getting to Know The Rules	73
16	'He's A Nice Chap to Play With'	78
17	Beating Your Opponent in Match-play	82
18	The Way to Low Scoring	86
19	Your Competition Day	90
20	Clinic	93
21	Doing Your Homework	102
22	Preparation for The 19th Hole	105
	Golfing Dictionary	114

MAX FAULKNER

ABOUT THE AUTHOR

MAX FAULKNER, born at Bexhill in 1916, is one of the most colourful golfers of our time. Son of Gus Faulkner, who was a golf professional of great ability, Max has won almost every major British title—including the British Open Championship, at Portrush in 1951. Currently he is the last Briton to have won this, the most coveted award in golf.

Faulkner has represented Great Britain in five Ryder Cup matches, including the victorious team which defeated the Americans at Lindrick in 1957.

Three times he has won the Spanish Open Championship; he was granted honorary membership of La Puerto de Herro Golf Club, in Madrid.

Among other interests, Faulkner is a keen sea-fisherman—and even to this sport he has introduced an element of typical drama. In 1950, while fishing off Selsey, Sussex, he dived into the sea to rescue two boys being swept away by the current.

Faulkner has said that his favourite golf shot is the drive with a following wind, and from a spectator's point of view there are few more inspiring sights than the Mighty Max, feet well apart, swinging with such glorious abandon.

Now, at 49, Faulkner is still the favourite of the crowds. Here are his tournament successes:

1937 Winner, Berkshire Championship
       Winner, Addington Foursomes
1938 Winner, Midland Open Championship
1946 Winner, Dunlop-Southport Tournament
1947 Winner, West of England Championship
       Ryder Cup Team

1949 Fourth, British Open Championship
      Winner, Dunlop Tournament
      Winner, Penfold Tournament
      Winner, Lotus Tournament
      Ryder Cup Team
1950 Fourth, British Open Championship
      Winner, Long-Driving Competition, Royal Mid-Surrey
1951 Winner, British Open Championship
      Winner, Dunlop Masters' Tournament
      Winner, Dunlop Tournament
      Winner, Long-Driving Competition, Sunningdale
      Winner, Long-Driving Competition, Brighton
      Winner, Long-Driving Competition, Bournemouth
      Ryder Cup Team
1952 Winner, Spanish Open Championship
      Winner, Dunlop Tournament
      Winner, Professional One-Round Tournament, New
          York
1953 Winner, 'News of the World' Match-Play Champion-
          ship
      Winner, Spanish Open Championship
      Ryder Cup Team
1954 Ninth, British Open Championship
      Winner, Surrey Open Championship
1957 Winner, Spanish Open Championship
      Sixth, British Open Championship
      Ryder Cup Team
1958 Sixth, British Open Championship
1959 Winner, Irish Hospitals £5000 Tournament
1962 Winner, Woodlawn International Tournament, W.
          Germany
1964 Winner, Southern Professional Championship
      Second, Dunlop Tournament
      Semi-finalist, 'News of the World' Match-Play
          Championship

FOREWORD

By George Houghton

THE most important part of every successful endeavour must be enthusiasm, and of all the golfing giants I know, none waxes more enthusiastic than Max Faulkner. For this reason alone, he was the right man to be chosen for this important book, designed to get beginners started in what the author calls 'the greatest game on earth'.

Anyone who doubts Max's enthusiasm should have seen him at Lindrick in 1957, when Great Britain defeated America for the Ryder Cup. Faulkner participated in the foursomes matches, but not in the singles. Nevertheless, he played a noble part in the great victory because his infectious zest spread to every member of the British team. With boundless energy, Max ran from match to match spurring on the side, and skipper Dai Rees was the first to say 'thank you'.

If Max Faulkner can't show you how to enjoy golf no one can and you must just decide to take up hop-scotch, or something.

Years ago, in Hertfordshire, we played as partners in a four-ball match. A fair crowd of club members followed us round and the effect of Max's play on all of us was tremendous. He was in his hey-day, drove with gusto and hit the ball incredible distances. Here was a man enjoying his golf; it was so obvious. There was abandon in his play, but his shots were beautifully disciplined. On that day, holing everything out, he finished two shots inside par on a golf course which he had never previously played!

At the age of forty-nine Max Faulkner is still on top, which means his methods are right. In this book he goes to infinite pains to pass them on and I have tried to illustrate his theories so that the beginner gets his golf right, from the start.

Faulkner rightly declares that proficiency is essential for the player to get full enjoyment from the game. He wants us all to have fun. In this book, I believe his enthusiasm rubs off.

THIS GLORIOUS GAME!

IF you have never golfed, I reckon you are missing the best thing in life.

Golf is for men and women of all ages; becoming a good player depends neither on physique nor a healthy bank balance.

This glorious game keeps you physically fit and mentally alert. Every shot needs care and concentration, so the worries and problems of your workaday life simply vanish. You go to lovely places and meet interesting people. In fact, you live an ideal, full life.

The handicapping system enables players of varying standards to compete on equal terms. Rabbits play tigers; octogenarians pit their skill against big-hitting youths.

Now, I may not be the best golfer the world has ever known, but I solemnly declare that not a single soul on earth enjoys the game more than I do. At the time of writing I am the last Briton to have won the British Open Championship. Now, thirteen years later, I have been assigned the task of finding and training a world-beater, and by the time this book is in your hands I hope some of my young men will already have given a good account of themselves. But what I am about to do in this book is equally important.

I propose to give you, who may never have played golf before, the proficiency you need to enjoy the fun. If, as a result of my text-book tuition, you get the same enjoyment I have had from the game you will be a happy man—and I will be well paid for my effort.

So long as you can stand, you can putt, and who is to say that you may not become the best putter in the world? All it needs is the trick, and practice.

But the greatest joy is hitting a golf ball hard, crisply and cleanly in such a way that it flies true, then rolls to rest more than two hundred yards away.

Why, then, when the world of golf has so many attractions to offer, do many people lose interest after a first attempt? The answer is: **Hitting a stationary ball is really more difficult than it seems.** Often, the potentially keen golfer gets so disheartened when trying to 'get the ball away' that he gives up in despair before he has even given the game a chance. What had appeared perfectly straightforward from a distance has now become disappointingly torturous.

No matter how keen the beginner is to get started, golf will only be enjoyed when the early frustrations have been overcome. That's where I come in. Study my book carefully. Your golf, right from the start, must be right.

Get cracking, and I guarantee you'll have fun as a *good* golfer.

Max Faulkner

1

MAKING A START—THE ARC

I BELIEVE that any normal man between fourteen and seventy can be taught to strike a golf ball more than two hundred yards.

There are two essentials. First, the ball must be struck square and flush with the centre of the golf clubhead. Second, at impact you need maximum clubhead speed.

Clubhead speed, zipp, is attained by timing and oomph!—which really means you must swing into a hit; so you must develop a sound golf swing on the correct plane. Success will largely depend on this, so the mechanism must be right.

Like handwriting, your swing must have 'style', then it will stand the test of time. Flowing naturally, golf will last for pleasurable years, and perhaps produce a few silver trophies for your mantelpiece.

Later I am going to deal with the mechanics of the swing, but at this point, before we get down to business, I would ask you to hold a golf club. Any club will do, and if you do not have one in the house, get one from the secondhand shop at the corner. Better still, ask the professional at your local golf club to fix you up. A rusty, hickory-shafted old thing will do but it should have a sound grip, because I want you to get the 'feel' of the swing. This way you will be able to go through the motions I describe.

First, I want you to conjure up the correct mental picture of a golf swing—this is a 'must' and should stay with you always.

Imagine that your club is a long-handled mallet. Now, let's suppose you are hammering a wedge under a door. The mallet must hit the wedge fair and square if it is to go flush under the door. In other words, from the time you start to take the mallet back to the moment it comes down again to strike the wedge, the path of the mallet-head is all-important. Also, by the time it makes contact it must have reached maximum speed.

If, on the backswing, you take the mallet **outside** the arc (that is to say, away from your body by straightening your right arm), you will strike a glancing blow, and the thin end of the wedge will probably be pushed right.

This is exactly what happens when you strike a golf ball from 'outside to inside'. The result is that the ball swerves in the air from left to right (this is called a 'slice', or 'banana' shot) and you lose distance.

In golf, we are actually striving for the reverse action. **To hit a long ball we must swing the club from 'in to out'. This means that the clubhead must be moving away from the body as it makes contact with the ball, from inside to outside the arc.** When struck correctly, the path of the ball through the air will bend slightly from right to left. This is called 'draw'.

As we progress, I will be talking a good deal about this 'in to out' movement. Time spent now getting a really clear picture will be well rewarded later.

From the wedge-under-the-door image, let us move a stage further.

We need a straight line; the edge of a carpet will do fine, or a floor-board. Now I want you to imagine that line as the direction in which you wish to hit a golf ball; we call it the 'line of flight'. Hold your club firmly with both hands (left hand near the top of the shaft and your right hand immediately under the left). Stand about two-and-a-half feet away from the straight line, with your feet about eighteen inches apart, and rest the club-head on the line. Tuck your right elbow comfortably into your right side so that the left shoulder is a little higher than the right. By moving only your arms and hands (don't bend your wrists or move the rest of your body) swing the club gently in pendulum fashion, about a yard either side of the imaginary ball. The

Preserving THE ARC

- START UNWINDING SLOWLY, HIPS FIRST. THIS TRANSFERS THE WEIGHT TO THE LEFT SIDE.

- DON'T OPEN CLUBFACE GOING BACK.

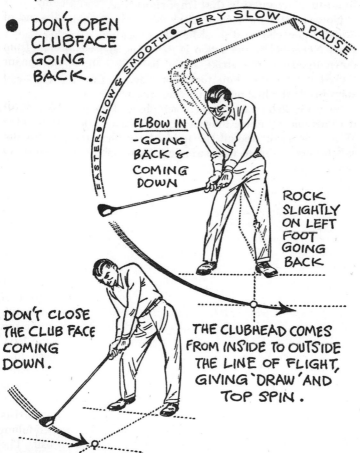

FASTER • SLOW & SMOOTH • VERY SLOW → PAUSE

ELBOW IN
- GOING
BACK &
COMING
DOWN

ROCK SLIGHTLY ON LEFT FOOT GOING BACK

DON'T CLOSE THE CLUB FACE COMING DOWN.

THE CLUBHEAD COMES FROM INSIDE TO OUTSIDE THE LINE OF FLIGHT, GIVING 'DRAW' AND TOP SPIN.

clubhead should lightly brush the line at the base of the swing.

If you carry out this operation correctly you will notice that the clubhead will stay **inside the line** on the backswing. This is what we are after. **Only the deliberate action of moving the right elbow away from the body will cause the clubhead to stray outside that important line.**

Now of course, when you take a full swing at a ball, as we shall do later, the clubhead must be taken back much farther than a yard. Nevertheless the action is the same, and when you swing down to make your strike at the ball the right elbow is still tucked comfortably into the right side, so that the clubhead stays inside the line until it makes contact.

Soon we shall piece together each phase of the golf swing until it forms one complete movement, and you will 'feel' it as such. When you have studied the finished product you will see the significance of 'in to out' swinging. Start off this way and you can't go wrong.

2

HOW TO HOLD THE CLUB AND 'FEEL'

PROFESSIONAL pianists take great care of their hands. So do professional golfers.

When shots start going astray, the first thing a golfer must do is look at his hands and check their position on the club.

In this game 'comfort' is vitally important—a comfortable grip; a comfortable stance. Unfortunately it is very easy to get comfortable in the wrong position. If you were to grip the club now without giving the matter any thought I dare say you would feel quite comfortable, but I doubt whether you could strike a golf ball successfully. What we have to do, therefore, is to develop the correct grip and then practise as much as possible until that grip becomes absolutely comfortable, more comfortable than any other way.

I use this word 'comfort' because I want to stress the importance of persevering with a grip which may feel unnatural at first.

As we proceed you will appreciate the importance of hands in the golf swing.

Everything depends on transmitting the power from your body—through the hands—to the clubhead.

Before we go into the mechanics of the grip, here are two gimmicks which will illustrate the hand-action we are looking for.

First, the left hand. With the palm face down, take it across the front of your body from left to right without bending your elbow too much. Then *crack* it smartly back as though you were breaking a rabbit's neck cleanly with the side of the hand. Do it four or five times, as hard as you can, and you will feel the power of the crack coming from your chest and shoulders, down your arm, to the side of your hand. The 'rabbit's neck' description may not be pleasant, but it will help you to remember, and that is the movement I want you to get.

Now the right hand. Simply imagine that you are cracking a whip from right to left in front of your body. Here, the power of the crack is stored up for the last six inches of the hand-movement. The hand goes back fairly slowly, then *crack*. Once again, you will feel the vibration of power coming down, through your shoulder and arm, to the wrist and hand.

Across the front of your body, with hands apart, carry out the two operations simultaneously so that the moment of *crack* is the same with both hands.

There you have it. This is the action of each hand that we must strive for. Once you have a clear mental picture of this movement, you are ready to grasp the club and have a go.

The type of grip I am going to recommend and describe is called the 'overlap'. This is what they call the orthodox way, although several of my fellow-professionals use other methods. My good friend, Dai Rees, for instance, holds the club the two-handed, non-overlap way—and no one can question his success with it. But Dai has rather small hands and short fingers, and that particular style suits him better.

For the 'overlap' grip, let the clubhead rest on the ground. Lay the shaft diagonally across the palm of the left hand. It should pass over the centre of the index finger, across the base of the second, and the top of the shaft should be half an inch beyond the outside edge of the hand. Now, close your left hand, with the thumb pointing down the shaft. Carefully move your hand round, without moving the club, until you can see the first two and a half knuckles. Your thumb should now lie towards the right of the shaft, still pointing straight down. You will notice that most of the top of the shaft is now hidden beneath your wrist.

Place the right hand on the club so that the little finger is round the knuckle of the left-hand index finger. Now grip the

.shaft with the right hand, so that the palm of it covers the left thumb. You will notice a V formed between the thumb and index finger of the right hand, and this should be pointing towards your right shoulder.

When you are quite sure that your hands are in their correct positions, swing the club gently and quite freely within the important 'in to out' arc so that you get the 'feel' of this grip. At first, it may be rather uncomfortable—you need time to get used to an unnatural position—but this is it for you in future. Never deviate from this grip and keep the 'feel' for ever.

Remember the 'rabbit's neck' and 'whip-cracking' demonstration. Although the two hands carry out different operations, they must function together with perfect co-ordination.

Here is an important point to remember: The golf arc and swing is mainly controlled by the left hand. When we analyse the swing closer you will see that it is **the downward pull of the left hand which governs the actual line of the clubhead.** The right hand is most active near the area of contact, to produce a good *crack* on the whip. If we allow the right hand to take over too much control at the beginning of the downswing, the hit will come from outside and the arc (which you will see in the illustration) will be spoilt.

At this point we must consider how tightly we should be gripping the club.

As I have said, the left hand makes the arc so must be in command. Therefore the left grip should be firm. The best description I have heard of the grip: Imagine that you are holding a child's hand as you cross a busy road. You don't want to hurt the child by gripping like a vice, but you must hold the hand firmly enough to stop the child from running away.

One final golden rule: **Never loosen your grip on the club at any time during the swing.** If you do, the head of the club will probably not return flush to the ball at the point of 'contact'.

When you are quite happy about the 'feel' and completely comfortable I shall consider that you have mastered the grip. You are ready to address the ball.

3

SETTING YOURSELF UP—THE STANCE

THE mechanics of striking a golf ball start from the moment you take a club from your bag. Actually, even earlier than that. Before you select a club, when you are walking up to make your shot, you should be working out the distance and direction; on this data depends the type of shot you must produce.

Then you adopt a stance.

This means that you take up a comfortable position for hitting the ball as intended. The way that you carry out this preliminary will have an important bearing on the success of the shot. Everything must be right.

I think the easiest way to give you the correct stance is to go through these main points:

Distance between the feet;
Position of the ball in relation to the feet;
Position of the feet in relation to the intended line of ball flight.

First, how far should the feet be apart? This is really going to depend on the shot you are playing. Generally speaking, for long shots they should be well apart, and closer up for the short game. When you are going all out to hit a long 'un it is important that you are well anchored to the ground. For these shots, I like to place my feet wider apart than the width of my shoulders. Balance is vital, and you can't keep your balance if your feet are too close together—particularly when the clubhead is travelling

20

HANDS & FEET

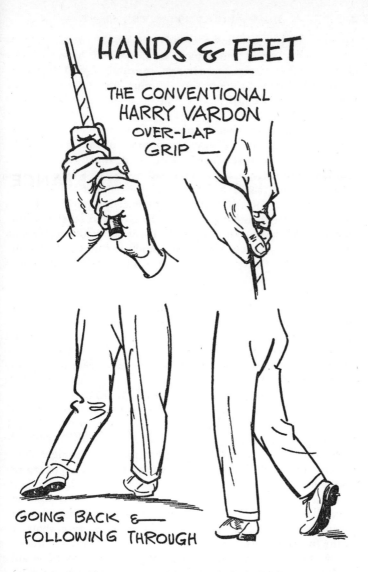

THE CONVENTIONAL
HARRY VARDON
OVER-LAP
GRIP —

GOING BACK &
FOLLOWING THROUGH

flat out. As you get closer to the target your backswing gets shorter and you will find it more comfortable to have your feet closer together. Even so, **always maintain good balance**. Cyril Tolley, one of the greatest amateurs, used to say that if he were to name one essential to all good golf shots he would decide on 'balance'.

Where should the feet be in relation to the ball? There are two positions we must check: the distance of the feet from the ball, and which foot should be nearer to it. Again, these factors are dependent on the shot. You will be farthest away for the long shots, and stand in 'cosier' as you approach the target. For most shots, address the ball approximately equi-distant from the feet. As I say, these points will be governed by the type of shot you are playing. In due course I will deal with each type in detail, but stick to these general rules and you won't go far wrong.

Third point: the position of the feet in relation to the line of flight.

You will hear golfers speak of the 'square stance'. This means quite simply that the feet (and the shoulders) are parallel with the intended line of ball flight. I might add here that the 'square stance' is easier to adopt on the living-room carpet than it is on the golf course. Out on the course, where the contours of the ground can be misleading, it is a very common fault to place the feet incorrectly. When in doubt use this trick. Take a club and place it along the ground immediately in front of your toes. Step back and you will soon see if the shaft is parallel to the line of flight. If the club points left, you are all set to take the club outside the arc, and when you strike, the ball is probably going to head towards the thick undergrowth to the right of the fairway. If the club points right, you're going to be in trouble on the left!

These, of course, are simple cardinal facts. When you have advanced in the game you will use these refinements for producing certain tricky shots. But first I want you to get grooved in the fundamentals.

Adopting a stance prior to making a golf shot is rather like checking the instrument panel before flying into space. Inspect the grip, left arm, position of the feet, pause, relax . . . then wind-up slowly for take-off.

I cannot too often repeat that **there must be no tension** as the club is taken back. This is anxiety-point No. 1 and even the most experienced players sometimes go wrong here. Tension locks the body into discomfort from which it is quite impossible to swing freely at the ball.

How do we make sure that the body is relaxed? Well, most important, see that your grip on the club is not too tight. A tight grip rises up the tendons of your wrists and arms into every muscle in your body. The right, 'sympathetic' grip will let the clubhead swing into the correct arc. Then, check that your knees are relaxed, slightly bent. This will enable you to get the top half of your body right round on the backswing, without swaying. You'll see what I mean in the next chapter.

There you are. If you have completely understood, you are now set up correctly to enjoy the fun and excitement of hitting a golf ball, sweetly and far.

4

WINDING UP THE BACKSWING

WHAT distinguishes a player's style? Many things, but largely it is a matter of how the player winds up, the way he takes the clubhead from the ball at the beginning of the backswing.

As a tournament professional for many years, it has been my life to play with the greatest golfers in the world. Half the fun has been watching styles and comparing notes with other professionals. We always say that if you want to make money at this game you've got to do your homework. After years of playing and studying I have no hesitation in advocating my own style—for me. It may also suit you, but in any case I am showing you how to assimilate the fundamentals which are right for everyone.

The important thing is that although styles vary, most top-line golfers 'come into' the ball the same way. Study any action photographs of famous golfers in the hitting area—when the club is about to make impact with the ball—and you will see that the positions of the strikers are almost identical. The players' heads are well down, the clubhead is moving at speed from inside to outside the line of flight, and the strikers are hitting hard against the left side of the body. This latter point will be elaborated later.

The great Belgian golfer, Flory Van Donck, for instance, has a very upright backswing. To get into the correct 'in to out' hitting position he has cultivated a very definite loop at the top of his swing. And there are other unorthodox backswingers.

But these men are experienced professionals and I would not advocate individual styles for you, a beginner.

The 'Max Method' ensures two things: The clubhead stays inside the line of the arc until contact has been made with the ball; at the top of the backswing the hands and arms are in a position from which they can pour into the clubhead a maximum of power.

The secret of my way is to **keep the clubhead as close to the ground as possible for the first three feet of the backswing. This will keep your left arm straight, but not stiff.**

Remember, please, that I am now pulling the swing to pieces so that you can slowly perform with your practice club. These instructions are the swing under a microscope. You must perform as directed, but later you will acquire the 'feel' of these movements, so that your 'muscle-memory' gets the club swinging the right way for best results.

I have never said that golf is easy, but it is tremendously worthwhile. Once you get going, I hope you will do what follows, naturally and easily. For the time being, here it is in detail.

Let's take the important wind-up.

First, adopt the stance for a long wood, or iron shot. The ball is midway between the feet. When the clubhead is placed on the ground behind the ball, the top of the shaft will be a hand-span from the crutch; your left arm will be straight; your right elbow will be bent and tucked comfortably near your right hip.

Now, by moving only the hands, arms and shoulders (don't bend or turn the wrists) in one piece, take the clubhead away from the ball on the inside of the arc until it has moved approximately one yard. The clubhead should still be close to the ground.

That is stage one, and the important thing to notice is that we have made no conscious effort to 'cock' the wrists which would take the clubhead away from the ground. We have kept well inside that magic line (which runs through the ball and is parallel to your toes). **The player's head has been kept perfectly still—it helps if you look at an imaginary spot one inch behind the ball.**

Stage two: The body begins to wind-up. This brings the clubhead round and up until it has travelled about six feet. Your left knee will begin to 'give' to the right, and your hips are turning; your right elbow is still close to your right hip, while your left shoulder is moving round under your chin.

Stage three: 'Break' your wrists and continue to turn the hips. **Your shoulders must make a maximum turn, until the left is immediately under your chin.** The clubhead will now have travelled over three-quarters of a circle and you have already generated tremendous 'body power'. This must now be controlled and unleashed into the hands.

You are now at the top of the swing, so let's review the situation as it should be at this moment. Your left heel will be slightly off the ground to allow your left knee to be bent towards the right—not outwards. Your right leg should be holding its original position, still slightly bent at the knee, but the right hip is well back. Your shoulders will have turned so that a spot between your shoulder-blades would point in the direction you intend to hit the ball. The right elbow must be pointing down, and still won't be far away from the side of your body.

I must continually emphasise that, throughout the entire swing, the head should be kept perfectly still. This ensures that your body does not sway. If your head moves, so do the shoulders, which can well put the whole body out of alignment. Then the clubhead will not maintain the correct path, and the 'strike' will be off-centre. A good way of checking whether your head is moving is to swing—without a club—with your forehead pressed against a wall. This also shows how much your body should be bent at the waist for the address, because you should be able to carry out the backswing quite comfortably this way.

Another point. You must be secure with the grip of your left hand. There must be no slackening. In an effort to swing the club right round you may find a tendency to release at the top. If you do, the club may turn in your hand, and this, too, will prevent the club-face from coming down 'square' to the ball. In other words, try to avoid the 'piccolo-player' action, which is what they call opening the left-hand grip at the top.

You will see exactly what I mean when you practise the whole backswing.

For every golf shot a good, firm base is essential. This means that your feet—possibly with the aid of spiked shoes—must grip the ground. On the wind-up, do not fall into the trap of letting your weight go to the right edge of the right foot. This temptation comes from an effort to turn the hips.

I have broken this operation down into three separate stages. But don't forget to work out the drill until you can *swing* back, round and up in **one complete movement**. Don't go in for exaggerated contortions. If you are over forty, don't attempt too much left shoulder 'dip' as you turn. In other words, swing flatter; you will still reach a good hitting position if you make a full turn of the shoulders and 'cock' the wrists at the top.

Hands, arms, shoulders and trunk must turn in one piece. Try first in slow motion, then gradually get swinging in such a way that at all times you can actually feel the weight of the clubhead, as if it was an apple swinging on a piece of string.

If your right knee is kept slightly bent, you will sense a definite **resistance** in the lower half of your body. This resistance, or coil, is the key to the downswing, which can be likened to the unwinding of a spring.

3 PAUSE POSITION

NOW FULLY WOUND UP. READY TO UNCOIL, STARTING WITH THE HIPS...

BACK FACES THE HOLE.

WEIGHT IS EVEN ON THE INSIDES OF BOTH FEET.

4 STARTING DOWN

HEAD ABSOLUTELY STILL, BEHIND THE BALL

HIPS ARE TURNING TO THE FRONT.

LEFT ELBOW IS WELL IN.

WEIGHT IS MOVING TO THE RIGHT..

7 UNDER & THROUGH

THE HIT IS AGAINST THE LEFT HIP....

THE HEAD IS STILL BEHIND WHERE THE BALL WAS...

8 AWAY

HEADLINE STILL HASN'T MOVED

EVERYTHING HAS BEEN POURED IN.

YOUR BELT BUCKLE FACES THE FLAG.

THE SOLE OF YOUR RIGHT SHOE IS EXPOSED.....
HANDS ARE HIGH...
YOUR BACK IS ARCHED

G.—3

5

SWINGING DOWN AND FOLLOWING THROUGH

The movement of the downswing starts in the left hip.

When you have the shoulders right round and the clubhead has travelled back as far as it will go without affecting the general balance of the body, you sense resistance from the hips downwards. The feet are firmly based, and although the left heel has raised a little to help the hips round, the turn limit has been reached. The shoulders and trunk want to return to the natural face-front position.

At the instance of full pivot, there is a subtle pause at the top, then the left hip makes the first move. It unwinds and the rest of the body follows. The weight is being transferred to the left foot; the right elbow is coming into the right side, and the shoulders are squaring up towards the front.

The hands, of course, have farther to travel. When the rest of the body is square, the left arm will still be at an angle of 45 degrees across the front of the body, and the wrists will still be 'broken' to the maximum.

Now the all-important zipp! as the hands bring the clubhead down. Remember the 'rabbit's-neck-and-whip-cracking' image. This is when it comes into action.

The only way really to get the 'feel' is to do the whole operation —backswing and downswing—in slow motion, stopping every few seconds as though you were posing for photographers. Speed up by degrees until the clubhead swings, and you can feel the torsion of the recoiling club-shaft, which is the elusive secret known as timing.

At point of impact, your left arm will be straight and almost in a line with the shaft of the club. Try and get the feeling of hitting against your left side. This is the leverage which whips the clubhead through with maximum speed.

Before proceeding to the final phase of the swing, please let these four essentials sink in. We have reached the point of your instruction when the permanent framework of your golf mechanism must be established.

1. **Throughout the swing your head must remain perfectly still.**
2. **Wind up slowly, in one piece.**
3. **In the downswing the clubhead must be moving from inside to outside. This will happen if your right elbow is tucked well in.**
4. **The weight of your body will be transferred automatically to your left leg without any conscious effort on your part.**

Now the follow-through. If you have followed the directions so far and the club is swinging correctly, you are bound to have a good follow-through. So forget it—let it ride freely. It is important that there should be no restriction. To put it my favourite way: **The best golf swing is DISCIPLINED ABANDON.**

The follow-through depends on what has gone before, but in your slow-motion exercises, this is what it should look like. At the point of impact the right arm straightens, so that for a brief time both arms are fully extended. **Your gaze should be fixed on the spot where the ball has been. The head must not move until the right shoulder is well and truly under the chin.**

The right heel will be off the ground now, and there will be a considerable amount of pressure against the left side. Don't let it collapse, but let the right hip swing round until the buckle of your belt faces the target.

By this time the ball will be travelling like a bullet. The momentum of your swing will have turned your body right round. But don't swivel the left foot or you won't hit against a firm left side—and if you think I am repeating myself you are quite right. I'll do anything that helps to make these points register.

How does the end of the swing look? The hands should be high; the sole of your right shoe should be exposed and everything except that sole should be facing the target; if the shot was a drive, the back should be slightly arched, because you have taken pains to be behind the ball at impact.

There you have it. That is the golf swing. I know that some will say I have cluttered you up with detail, but this has been deliberate at this stage of your tuition. I am hoping that you are assuming the various postures (preferably before a large mirror) as I describe them. But remember, you must **turn it all into a golf swing, and establish 'muscle-memory' until the movements are uncomfortable when you do them incorrectly.**

6

TIMING—THE GREAT SECRET

So far, you have been playing 'indoor golf'; going through the motions of the golf swing. Soon I will be showing you how to play each type of shot. But before I do, there is another aspect of the swing which you should understand. The secret of good timing is the most important thing about the actual strike. Unfortunately, it cannot be photographed, nor can it be adequately described. It can only be felt.

Everyone, from tap-dancers and ballerinas to steeplejacks and racing-drivers, must develop keen timing-sense. In golf, timing means **storing up the power of your swing, then unleashing it at exactly the right moment**.

Some folk are lucky enough to have been born with a natural sense of timing. Cricketer Ted Dexter, for example, could have just as easily become an international golfer. Another, Tom Graveney, is an above-average golfer. These men, and scores like them, are what we call 'naturals'; they can turn their hands to almost any ball game because they have an inborn sense of timing. Soon you will know if you are one of the lucky ones. If you are a 'natural' then this chapter is not for you. Master the mechanics, and the rest of the game will come easily.

Very few non-regular sportsmen are 'naturals', but don't let that put you off. With most golfers, good timing is developed after practice. And there are two rules that will help.

In the previous chapter I mentioned the 'subtle pause' at the top of the backswing. This is secret No. 1.

33

A common fault, particularly with beginners, is to take the club back too quickly and then hit the ball without pausing. Usually this is done because the newcomer to the game is naturally nervous at first, and he thinks that the sooner he can get the swing over and done with the better. But the result is that the arms and hands have swung at the ball before the rest of the body has had a chance to join in. In other words, the swing is finished long before the power from the body has been accumulated.

My advice is: **Take the club back slowly, then pause for a full second at the top before you start coming down. This gives you time to 'get a focus' on the ball. Count as you wind up: one, two, and (that is the pause) three— crack!** Come down as fast as you like—the faster the better—so long as you have started the movement with the hips (not the hands) and your right elbow doesn't stray from your side. The actual uncoiling of the 'spring' of your wound-up body will get you going, so that the speed of the clubhead increases and 'rushes' through the resistance of the ball.

Secret No. 2 is 'rhythm'. This means that **nothing in the swing must be jerky. You must go back smoothly, until the left shoulder is under your chin.**

One can only describe the mechanics of the swing. You've got to feel the swing in motion, and you will soon know if the feel is right or wrong.

Once again: All this golf-swing mechanism must be practised repeatedly until 'muscle-memory' takes over.

One of our promising young tennis stars, surprisingly beaten by an unknown opponent, was asked to explain her defeat. She replied: 'I suddenly began to *think* about what I was doing.'

I see her point, and it clearly illustrates what I mean by 'muscle-memory'. Instead of playing her natural, flowing game— hitting every shot with unconscious ease—she started to 'tense up'. Soon she lost her stride. What had hitherto been effortless, now became laboured. In other words, her *rhythm* had gone, and *timing* went with it. She began to 'place' the racket, instead of relying on 'muscle-memory'.

TO BE
AVOIDED

THE FATAL
OUT TO IN
___
THE CLUBHEAD
STRIKES WITH
A GLANCING
BLOW — THE
BALL 'SLICES'
TO THE RIGHT
AND QUICKLY
STOPS.

TO BE
ACQUIRED

IN TO OUT
- The power
shot ...

THE RIGHT
ELBOW IS
TUCKED IN
SO THE ARC
IS CORRECT.

THE BALL
'DRAWS' TO
THE LEFT
WITH PLENTY
OF 'RUN'

Watch a long-distance runner in peak condition, and you will see the rhythm of his action. Quite unconsciously, he seems to be putting 'poetry' into every stride.

Remember that word 'poetry'—it's the best way I know of describing rhythm. Out on the golf course, try humming a Strauss waltz; you would be surprised if you knew how many top players do just that, when they feel themselves becoming jerky!

In good golf, everything must be right. Often the slightest thing can upset rhythm, and I don't mean only when you are swinging a club. A bad shot can ruin your rhythm for three or four holes—if you let it. Arriving a few minutes late for your game can prevent you getting into rhythm; or a talkative opponent can have the same effect. Later I will be dealing with the mental side of the game and will elaborate on these points. For the time being, remember that **rhythm means doing everything at a regular, smooth pace**. If, right at the start of your golfing career, you can get into the habit of doing things smoothly (and this means not getting flustered when you hit a bad shot) you will soon develop rhythm—and in due course, if you also remember the 'subtle pause' at the top of the backswing, timing will follow.

7

CHOOSING CLUBS

You needn't be a millionaire, or even well-to-do, to get fun from golf.

For a modest outlay you can be quite adequately equipped.

If you watch some of golf's elder statesmen—men who have been playing the game for fifty years or more—you will see that many still perform really well with no more than half a dozen clubs.

Times change, but the game is fundamentally the same. In the old days clubs had delightful names. Today, these have made way for impersonal numbers—but the object is still to get the ball into the hole in as few shots as possible.

The modern set of golf clubs comprises four woods, nine irons, and a putter. If money is no object (which, let's face it, is unlikely) you may want to start off with the full quota. This is pleasant, but unnecessary.

In 1964, a well-known firm had the ingenious idea of sponsoring an annual 'seven-clubs-only' tournament for professionals. It has become one of the highlights of our season. All competitors (most of whom usually play with the maximum fourteen clubs) are restricted to seven, and the results are astonishing. Taking away half our armoury has made hardly any difference to the scores!

I am going to suggest, therefore, that you start with only seven clubs. One of the secrets of this game is to keep it as simple as possible. If you can master seven clubs (and that must surely be easier than fourteen) I guarantee you will be a match for anyone.

Before deciding on which seven clubs to choose, I will go through the range.

First, the four woods: The number one, or driver, is used exclusively for driving from a tee-peg. It has almost no loft (angle of the club-face in relation to the shaft) and is the longest-shafted club in the bag. The average golfer, from a tee-peg, should be capable of hitting the ball more than two hundred yards.

The two-wood (once called a 'brassie') is used for long shots from the fairway. It has slightly more loft than a driver, and in fact many players take a two-wood from the tee when their driving is going through a bad spell. The added loft makes it easier to get the ball up, but you may not get so much run on the ball after it has landed.

The three-wood (or spoon) has more loft and this is also used for long shots from the fairway. The four-wood is used from the fairway when the surface is not so good, or the rough when you have a good 'lie'.

Now the irons. Once again, the higher the number the more loft there is on the club-face, and the higher will be the trajectory of the ball in flight.

Most sets of clubs start with the two-iron. This is difficult to use, particularly for beginners, for it has only a slight loft. Professionals often take a two-iron from the tee when accuracy is more important than length. But mostly it is a fairway club, used when the ball is 'sitting up'. A good two-iron shot will send the ball about as far as a three- or four-wood, and most golfers rightly use one or other of the latter because it is easier.

The three-iron is for shots of about 160 yards. On most courses there are five or six holes of between 350 and 400 yards, and the average player will find a three-iron most useful for playing approach shots to these greens. Of course, I must not generalize on distances. The lengths which you are likely to achieve will depend on many factors. You may develop into a really big-hitter, in which case you will use one or two clubs higher than I am indicating. On the other hand, you may be taking up the game rather late in life, and these distances will be beyond your scope. Don't worry. I mention them only as a guide, and don't forget that **it is better to be on the green with a three-iron than short with a five. Don't allow pride to induce you to take less club than you really need.**

Next come the 'mid-irons', the four, five and six, lofted for shots of about 150, 140 and 130 yards, and the 'short-irons'— seven, eight and nine—for 120 yards and under to the green. Some of the 'short-irons' are used also for recovery shots from sand or rough, or to overcome obstacles 'twixt you and the target.

The nine-iron is usually the 'sand-blaster', a deep-faced, flat-soled and well-lofted club for getting out of deep bunkers.

Finally, there is the putter, which is used more than any other club in the bag.

That is the complete set. From time to time you may hear of a one-iron, ten-iron or five-wood. These need not concern us for the moment. The rules stipulate a maximum of fourteen, but for you, the beginner, my tip is seven.

Which clubs should be chosen? Well, you must be equipped for every aspect of the game: long, medium and short shots, and, of course, the hazards.

Also in your bag there must be a putter. Later, when I have dealt thoroughly with the techniques of this department of the game, you will see the importance of choosing the right putter. This does not necessarily mean buying a new one. On the contrary, often an old putter, handed down from generation to generation, will feel more comfortable. Bobby Locke, four times winner of the Open Championship, was one of the greatest exponents on the greens, and he used an old hickory-shafted putter that his father gave him when he was a boy. Good putters, like wine, often mature with age—and the rust doesn't encourage the glinting sun.

You must carry a wooden club for driving. The number one is preferable for extra length, but you may find a two-wood, with a little loft, easier at first.

Then I suggest a second wood, either a three or four. The four-wood is a versatile club and I suggest it because it can cope with a wider range, and the yard or two you lose in length does not matter.

To complete your first 'set', choose the odd-numbered irons; the three-, five- and seven-iron for long and middle-distance shots, and the nine-iron for short pitch-shots and bunkers.

That is all you need to make a start.

Apart from making your introduction to the game simpler, restricting yourself to seven clubs greatly reduces the initial outlay. Good, secondhand steel-shafted clubs are easy to come by. Make sure, however, that you buy good ones; cheap, old-fashioned (thin-bladed) clubs are no economy. Any professional will advise.

You have your seven clubs, a few wooden tees and half a dozen old (or repainted) golf balls. Now, find a quiet stretch of grass . . .

8

HOW TO HIT THE LONG 'UNS!

LET me say right away, there is no short cut to good golf. If you are about to try to hit a golf ball for the first time in your life, don't despair if you miss it! Not a soul on earth can expect to hit more than two or three good shots first time out. But persevere now and you'll be thankful later.

When you have found a piece of level ground with a good wide fairway ahead, you are ready to set yourself up for THE DRIVE.

There are two important differences between swinging in the comfort of your own home and actually hitting a golf ball.

To begin with, there is the **psychological effect.** Try not to get 'tensed up'—keep as relaxed as possible the whole time. It helps if you flex the knees and breathe deeply before you swing.

Secondly, there is the **resistance of the ball at point of impact.** Hit through the ball and remember to finish the swing with your hands as high as possible. There will be a tendency to 'stab' at the ball. Avoid this; just 'sweep' it away.

Before you actually stand up to the ball to make your strike, swing your club freely once or twice to get the 'feel'. Then, when quite relaxed, tee the ball up so that it stands about an inch from the ground. A couple more swings at nothing, then you are ready.

For the drive, the ball should be opposite your left heel. Your feet will be wide apart—wider than the width of your shoulders. Don't reach for the ball but get yourself into a

comfortable position so that your left arm is straight and making
a straight line with the club. This means your left shoulder is at
least a couple of inches higher than your right. Remember the
grip, and make sure that it is firm with the left hand, and gentle
with the right. The V formed by the thumb and index finger of
the right hand should be pointing straight towards your right
shoulder. Take aim at an object on the skyline and move your
feet until they are absolutely parallel with the intended line of
flight.

The fact that the ball is opposite your left foot means that
'contact' is actually made *after* the clubhead has reached the
bottom of the arc (i.e. slightly on the up-swing). When struck
correctly this will put top-spin on the ball and make it run
merrily along when it hits the ground. **Keep your body behind
the ball at impact—this will happen if you keep your
head perfectly still until you have hit through the ball.**
This isn't easy, and one is inclined to restrict the 'through the
ball' action by concentrating too hard on being behind the ball.
If you think of making the right shoulder 'ride' under the chin it
will help.

I can almost hear you saying, 'There's an awful lot to
remember'. There is of course, but don't forget that 'muscle-
memory' will take over the details after practice. When you are
over these first hurdles you will be well on the way to playing
good golf.

Here is the sequence of events for the drive:

1. **Having teed the ball, establish the intended line of
   flight.**
2. **Check that the feet are 'square' and that your grip
   shows the V's pointing to the right shoulder.**
3. **Left arm is straight, right elbow is close to right
   side.**
4. **Hands, arms, shoulders and body turn in one piece.**
5. **Clubhead stays close to the ground for nearly a
   yard, and inside the line.**

HOW MAX SETS UP FOR THE LONG ONE

● HE LIKES TO SWEEP THE BALL OFF THE TEE WITH A <u>LONG-SHAFTED</u>, <u>DEEP-FACED</u> DRIVER.

● HIS HEAD IS WELL <u>BEHIND THE BALL</u> AND VERY STILL.

● THE BALL IS <u>TEED HIGH</u>.

● THE STANCE IS <u>WIDER</u> THAN THE SHOULDERS.

● THE LEFT ARM AND CLUB MAKE <u>A STRAIGHT LINE FROM SHOULDER TO BALL</u> AND SHOULD BE LIKE THIS AT IMPACT.

● THE RIGHT ELBOW IS <u>TUCKED IN</u> TO TAKE THE CLUB AROUND <u>CLOSE TO THE GROUND</u>.

6. Left shoulder turns under the chin until your back faces the target.

7. Pause for a second at the top.

8. Let the uncoiling of the body bring the arms and club down.

9. Keep the left side firm and the right elbow 'brushing' the right side.

10. Hit right through the ball, in to out, with both hands.

11. Don't look up until after your right shoulder is well under the chin, and the buckle of your belt faces the target.

12. Finish on a smooth swivel; hands high; sole of the right shoe fully exposed to the right; weight on the left foot, but the whole body behind the spot where the ball was teed.

These are your twelve pointers to successful driving. Read them every night before you turn out the light, and repeat them to yourself on your way to the office in the morning. And when you are an experienced golfer, keep my 'golden rules' in a handy place for when things go wrong.

That is the Drive, and don't despair if mastering it takes time. The big 'un is the shot from which you will get most fun, and when you've got it working, the blood, sweat and tears will have been worthwhile.

For all wooden club shots the same dozen rules apply (although of course, the ball is only teed-up for the drive). For the long fairway shots, the ball should still be in a position almost opposite the left foot, to ensure that you put the weight of your body behind the shot at impact.

Try never to scoop the ball into the air. The clubs are angled for all the lift you require. For these long shots, the trajectory of the ball in flight should not be too high. We are after a fairly low flight so that the ball hits the ground at a shallow angle and runs powerfully along the ground after pitching. The high ball loses distance because it stops quicker.

One final word before you get down to hard practice:

I believe that golf is mainly a left-handed game. The right hand comes in for that important split-second before impact. Most good golfers develop their left side more than the right. That's why my left shoulder is permanently an inch and a half higher than my right.

9

NOW FOR THE IRONS

Accuracy is the key word when talking about iron-shots. As you approach the green, judgement and control become more essential. Between your ball and the hole there lurk bunkers and all kinds of trouble. You must learn to avoid them.

Here is the big difference between a moderate golfer and a really good one. Often you will see an average golfer hitting the ball vast distances from the tee; but if he can't control his irons then he is wasting the length he has achieved with his driver. The good golfer makes use of length (or makes up for his lack of it) by playing accurate iron-shots.

Writing about the drive I used the word 'sweep' to describe the action of striking the ball from the tee. With irons, a better word is 'squeeze'. I'll explain.

If you squeeze an orange-pip between your fingers, it flies off just as your fingers come together. The same thing happens when the golf ball is 'squeezed' between the club-face and the ground. You'll remember that the club-face struck the drive *after* reaching the bottom of the arc—slightly on the upswing. For iron-shots, contact is made just as the clubhead reaches the bottom of the arc. With the drive, the clubhead brushed the ground a fraction before contact, and the result was that you put top-spin on the ball. With the irons, it's the reverse: **the blade of the clubhead comes down on the ball, then cuts through the ground,** and the angle depends on the shot you need. The clubs are angled to raise the ball; they range from No. 2 to

No. 9. The latter in the hands of an experienced golfer produces a 'parabola', angled astonishingly.

For the time being, simply make sure that the clubhead makes contact with the ball **before** the ground, not vice versa. That is the main difference between the drive and the iron-club shot.

Now we come to the stance. Near the target, you stand closer to the ball, and you will never be far wrong if you take all irons with the ball equi-distant from the feet. Make sure that the sole of the clubhead is flat on the ground, and that you stand just far enough away to keep your left arm fairly straight, but see that your right elbow is close to your right side. I must have mentioned that right elbow at least a dozen times! Bear with me, because it's so important. By keeping it in, you are ensuring that the clubhead does not stray outside that vital line.

Keep referring to my twelve golden 'musts' of the previous chapter; they refer to irons as well as to woods.

In time, when you begin to master the shots, you will take divots with the irons. These will be immediately in front of where the ball was, and they are your guide to the 'in to out' movement. If, when you have played a shot, the divot scar points slightly to the right, then you have played it correctly. If the scar points to the left, this is a sure sign that your right elbow has wandered, and you have struck from 'out to in'.

I'm no poet, but this may help to remind you:

> In golf, of course, the greatest sin
> Is playing all shots 'out to in';
> The greatest virtue lies, no doubt,
> In playing all shots 'in to out'!

When you are playing a full-blooded three-iron shot of, say, 160 yards, you will need a full swing, with the hands, arms and shoulders rotating as with a driver. But as you approach the green, your hands will not usually go quite so far up on the backswing. For the five- and seven-iron shots you will find that you can generate enough power by taking your hands round until they are just shoulder-high on the backswing. But remember, please, that the shoulders must also turn and the downswing still starts with the uncoiling of the body, hips first.

Don't make too much effort to get the ball in the air—the loft of the club does that. Also, at this stage, don't worry about length. That will come in due course, when you have clearly understood the various forces involved. One of the biggest mistakes which even experienced golfers make is to try and force a five-iron to go as far as a three. Too many players expect to excel too often; in trying to hit the ball out of sight, they over-swing. Hit the ball hard, yes, but don't over-swing. If you do, you will almost certainly lose balance and the chances are that you will hit the ground before the ball.

Start off your irons practice-session with a No. 7. This club has plenty of loft, so there won't be too much temptation to scoop the ball in the air. Remember the points emphasised during the indoor sessions, and let the swing come naturally. When you are hitting the ball straight, between 80 and 120 yards, take a No. 5, then a No. 3, and continue to go for accuracy, not length. Length will come later, almost without trying.

Remember, one can only 'feel' the golf swing; one can't describe it satisfactorily. Scores of books have been written on swing-theory; these are for you when you have advanced in the game. For the time being, there is no real substitute to good hard practice. If you have assimilated the mechanism, and beads of perspiration are appearing on your brow with sustained practice, you are well on the way to becoming a good golfer. What is more important—you are getting the right kind of fun from the game.

10

NEAR THE GREEN—HOW TO PLAY MATCH-WINNERS

WHEN I won the British Open Championship at Portrush in 1951, my short game was red hot.

There were plenty of players in the field driving as far as I was, but when it came to shots of one hundred yards and under, I usually had the edge.

Never before, nor since, have I consistently hit those shots better than I did throughout the four rounds of the '51 Championship. If I needed proof here it was. **The man who can master the short game takes the prize-money.** Of course it doesn't always click, even when your short game is good. Everyone knows that a few long, lucky putts often decides the issue, but usually the chap who is playing the most accurate approach-shots will take fewer putts during the round.

The object of every golf shot is to get the ball as near to the hole as possible—preferably in it, but failing that, near enough so that on the green only one putt will be necessary. This is easier said than done. Most golfers are well pleased if they take as few as thirty putts in a round of eighteen holes. There's no doubt, though, that the number of putts mostly depends on short-game accuracy, and needless to say, I was more than pleased when, in the four rounds of the '51 Open, I took 23, 27, 29 and 29 putts. So you see, it is vital that the low-handicap player gets within one-putt distance as often as possible from a hundred yards, or less.

The PITCH and RUN shot

PLAYED FROM CUT GRASS WITH A 5-IRON
-UPRIGHT OPEN STANCE -RIGHT ELBOW CLOSE
TO HIP - BOTH FEET FIRM - HEAD
STILL - ARMS STRAIGHT, NOT STIFF

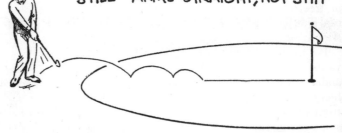

The CHIP shot
FROM ROUGH, OVER A HAZARD

-PLAYED WITH A 9-IRON OFF THE RIGHT FOOT-
BOTH FEET FIRMLY ON THE GROUND THROUGHOUT
-PLENTY OF HAND ACTION IN THIS SHOT-
HEAD IS DEAD-STILL 'TIL THE BALL IS ON ITS WAY

When you are near the green, there are two types of shots you must learn to play: the **pitch** and the **chip.** They require different techniques, so I will deal with them separately.

The idea of the **pitch-shot** is to get the ball high in the air, so that it lands on the green almost vertically and has enough back-spin to prevent it from rolling too far past the flag. The shot can be played when there is some sort of hazard—a bunker or tree, perhaps—between the ball and the hole. Usually you can pitch with a nine-iron from any distance between ten and a hundred yards.

For the full pitch-shot—that is to say about eighty to a hundred yards—you need a full swing, with the feet quite wide apart, and a full body turn. The ball should be equi-distant from the feet (i.e. in the midway position), though some prefer to play it from slightly right of centre. Make sure that your right elbow is still comfortably close to the right side, and that the left arm is straight. On the backswing, again make certain that you take the club inside the line—as for every other shot you have learned. At the top of the backswing, the hands should be about shoulder-height, ready to swing down into the hitting position. Again, I remind you to keep a firm grip on the club at the top—this, as I've said, is important for every shot, but even more so for the 'shorties' when accuracy counts most.

As with the other irons, the strike is made just before the clubhead reaches the base of its arc; ball first, then the ground. Once in the hitting area, the hands snap through and the club-face puts back-spin on the ball. The divot-scar should be pointing slightly right, indicating that you have hit from 'in to out'.

Hit right through with your head kept well down, and finish the swing with the hands high.

Nearer to the green (assuming there is a hazard) you play a similar shot, with refinements. The body takes less part in the swing. Stand with the feet a little closer together (but still maintaining good balance). Take the clubhead back so that the full cock of the wrists takes it about waist-high, but this time don't raise the left heel. You must keep the body absolutely still, and you do not need a full turn. But stick to the rule: hit from 'in to out' by keeping the right elbow tucked in.

There will be a tendency, as you play from shorter lengths, to be short. Don't be timid; try to get into the habit of 'flicking' these pitch-shots well up to the flag. It is always better to be past the hole than short of it. Practise playing over a bunker— this will help you to learn to play the ball well up to the hole.

The **chip-shot** calls for a different club and a different technique. It is quite straightforward; used when there is no bunker or hazard to negotiate and you are close to the putting surface. The idea is to chip the ball with a low trajectory so that, when it pitches, the ball runs along the ground to the hole. We don't want the ball to go high in the air, so we take a club with less loft. I suggest a five-iron.

For better control, the club is held further down the shaft. No body-movement is wanted for this shot—just arms and hands —so the feet will be quite close together. Try not to over-swing; the clubhead should travel back no more than two or three feet, so don't over-cock the wrists. The head must be kept still (this is important, for movement of the head changes the body position). Try to give the ball a smart rap. Forget about the follow-through, for if you have taken the club back correctly with a firm grip, the follow-through will take care of itself. Make sure, however, that you don't stab at the ball. The sole of the clubhead should just brush the grass as the strike is made.

Wise golfers practise these twenty- to thirty-yarders just as much as they practise long shots. Believe me, the 'shorties' can be life-savers. If the rest of your game is suspect, you can redeem the situation and still come in with a good score if you play them well. Quite often, amateurs completely ignore this department and when they are faced with a delicate pitch, or chip-shot, they just aren't good enough.

So practise the short game in your back garden until the cows come home. You'll steal a march on your friends, and win the half-crowns.

Sport & General

Flat out at Wentworth!
I was pleased with this drive from the 1st tee in a Daks Tournament.
Worth noting: I hit through the ball, but took care to keep my left side firm. High hands, and belt buckle facing the hole. Particularly good balance.

Photos: Topix

This is the position you should try to get at the top of the wind-up. Note: my shoulders have fully turned to be square to the direction I intend the ball to go; my left-hand grip on the club is very firm, and although there is a full pivot, my right elbow points to the ground and never gets far from my side.

Just for laughs, the bottom photo shows the piccolo grip— to be avoided at all costs. Purposely I have done everything wrong for this picture.

Sport & General

Another full-out tee shot, this time on the long 17th at Wentworth in the Dunlop Tournament. Picture shows my bearded caddie who became a familiar personality at the tournaments.

The drive does not always call for distance, and the lower photograph shows me 'taking care' and finishing with good balance on the short 2nd, also at Wentworth. This one was important; I took an eight iron and was satisfied with the result because the shot helped me to win the Dunlop Tournament.

Sport & General

This photograph illustrates what I said at the beginning
of the book. Golf is full of fun. Just look at the expressions
on the faces of these happy spectators. Lindrick, Yorkshire,
in 1957, and we have just won the Ryder Cup from the
Americans—the first time for twenty-four years!

I was thrilled to be in the British team. This picture, one
of the most treasured I possess, shows me congratulating
Dai Rees, our skipper, who played such a great part in us
winning 7 games against their 4.

Associated Press photo

United Press Inter

Trouble—often with a capital T, can be encountered in any round of golf. You must have the shots in your armoury ready to bring out when needed.

Before our Ryder Cup match at Lindrick, a game was arranged against top amateurs as a practice spin. I partnered Peter Alliss and once found our ball in this mess! With a sand-blaster there was no problem. I opened the face and took care to hit through. Bunkers and deep grass are not the menace they were before the flat-soled, heavy blasters and wedges were invented in the late thirties.

Sport & General

Heather is the toughest hazard of all. Getting out must be the first consideration; don't expect any distance, it is virtually impossible against dense growth. The above shows me playing from a particularly stubborn lie in heavy wet heather on the Berkshire Course, where the heather calls for excellent 'target golf' at all times.

The bottom photo shows a shot from St. Andrews rough which I had to play to reach the fourth green. There is plenty of rough at St. Andrews and always much controversy about the 'fairness' of the hazards which are not always visible from the tee. Nevertheless, most serious players agree that the 'Old' course at St. Andrews is golf's great 'examination paper'.

When playing from the rough or bunkers: First, keep your head particularly still; secondly, remember to hit through the ball—don't quit, or stab.

United Press International

Topi

'Drive for show, putt for dough', is what the Americans say. Of course, they are right. The long putt has often been described as the hardest shot in golf. You must be near enough to make the next one simple, and that is seldom easy.

Personally, I try to eliminate things that can go wrong when the heat is on. Get comfortable; avoid tension; don't move your head, even a fraction, or the shot is spoilt; try to watch the clubhead actually strike the ball; remember, practice makes—well, not perfect, perhaps, but it helps. If the hole dodges you for weeks on end, give your putter a rest. Try another; it may be kinder—for a while. Sometimes I even change my style of putting.

Work it out for yourself. There is no foolproof method that never fails.

11

PUTTING—A GAME WITHIN A GAME

Nearly half the shots played during a round of golf are putts. Yet no one, not even the greatest golfers who ever lived, has really mastered the secret of perfect putting. It would be accurate to state that if a player could be found who never missed a putt from less than ten feet he would be a world-beater.

We all have days when we think we have found the secret, but ten to one it has gone the very next day. Most of us are satisfied with an average of slightly under two putts per hole during a round.

What we must do is develop a 'safe' long-putting style which ensures that the ball finishes close to the hole every time; the chances are that some of the putts will drop.

Golf is a highly individual game. No two golfers putt the same way; most people, in their search for the secret, develop a style based on a hunch. Mr. John Blackwell, who was runner-up in the 1963 Amateur Championship, plays the other shots in an orthodox manner, but on the greens he holds his putter with his left hand below the right. This, he claims, obviates a tendency to 'twitch'. Joe Carr, brilliant Irish amateur, was having a bad spell and decided he could do better with a three-iron. But that also went sour and Joe returned to his putter. Arnold Palmer putts in knock-kneed fashion, to overcome a tendency to move the body, yet even Palmer has been known to miss short putts. In fact, almost every golfer you can name has some 'trick' which he believes is an aid to solving his problems.

When I was writing about the golf swing I mentioned that all great players 'come into' the ball the same way, even though their backswings are different. With putting, nothing need be standardised. Some believe in a long, smooth backswing; others say the shorter the better, with less margin for error. Some players are 'wristy'; others are stiff. As you gain experience you will develop a particular style. All I want to do at this stage is to give you pointers which will help you to carry out your own experiments. You'll have fun trying to find the secret. Who knows, you may even be successful.

To begin with, what about the club? I have already mentioned the importance of finding a putter that suits you. When you have selected, persevere. Don't immediately blame the putter when things start going wrong. I know from experience. In my time I have amassed one of the biggest collections of putters in the world. Until recently, when I lost my form on the greens I would go out and buy another putter. Now I know that mastering the art is not as simple as that. I've tried putting with nearly every shape of club ever put on the market; I've experimented with all techniques. After many years at the game, I have finally decided that it's the man, not the putter, that really counts. So take my advice, choose a comfortable, well-balanced putter and stick to it.

Having found a good putter, the next thing to do is find the 'sweet spot'. This means the exact spot on the club-face which is right geometrically for making contact with the ball. On some putters it will be dead centre of the face, but this is not always the case. The way to find out is to hold the club by the end of the grip with the thumb and forefinger of the left hand, letting the clubhead dangle freely. Then tap the face of the putter with a golf ball. When you can tap without feeling vibration in the fingers of the left hand, that is the 'sweet spot'. A good idea is to mark the top of the blade at that spot, so that you can line up the ball correctly at address. Some of the modern putters already have a mark to show the position of the 'sweet spot', but you may prefer to buy an old club, and marking the 'sweet spot' will be helpful.

You will want to experiment, and you must. But first, adopt a method which helps with these objectives: **Each putt must be struck with the correct strength; the ball must go in the direction you intend; your method must serve for any length of putt on any type of green.**

If you mastered these three points, you would hole every putt. Let's face it, this is unlikely, so try to master at least one of them. What you must avoid, if you are to score well, is taking three putts on any green. If you can putt with the correct strength, the chances are that you will always put your ball close enough to hole out with your second putt. Strangely enough, distance from the hole after the first putt is determined more on *strength* than direction. Experience will show that you are seldom far off line, but strength is something different.

So, of the three requisites, strength is the most important. Remember, it is a good fault to finish *past* the hole. Don't be short. The strong putt gives the hole a chance. From time to time you will hear golfers use this expression: 'Never up—never in.' On the greens, this is good wisdom.

The second requisite is 'direction'. This you get by keeping the face of the putter absolutely square to the intended line. This can be done if you keep a firm (but never tight) grip on the putter. My advice is **take the blade of the putter back without turning the wrists. Above all, keep your body perfectly still.**

Next, try and develop a style with which you can putt equally well from three to thirty feet. The action should be the same, although for a long putt you may take the club a little farther back.

After much trial and error, I can claim to be a reasonably good putter. My style suits me, and it may help to get you started.

For every putt, no matter what length, I stand upright; feet together, head over the ball. In keeping with my theory that golf is a left-handed game, I eliminate the use of my right hand by overlapping the left with all but the index finger and thumb of the right hand. Thumbs are together, and point straight down

THE 'MAX' METHOD
on the GREENS

- FIRST, THE STANCE IS UPRIGHT – SO THE PUTTER HAS A LONG SHAFT.

- FEET SHOULD BE CLOSE TOGETHER.

- A FIRM, LEFT-HAND GRIP WITH THREE FINGERS OF THE RIGHT OVERLAPPING THE LEFT. THUMBS IN LINE DOWN THE SHAFT.

- HEAD IS <u>VERY</u> STILL.

- CLUB IS TAKEN BACK SLOWLY, CLOSE TO GROUND, ON DIRECTION LINE, FOR <u>10 INCHES</u>

  AND GOES THROUGH FOR <u>4 INCHES</u>.

the shaft. I am not afraid of cocking my wrists on the backswing, but I always make sure that the head of the club goes back on the line of the putt. Contact with the ball is a smart 'rap'; the strength of the 'rap' depending on the length of the putt.

The important thing about my own style is that I try not to overdo the follow-through. My opinion is, the more you follow-through the greater your chance of losing the line of the putt. So I make a deliberate effort to stop the clubhead almost as soon as it has struck the ball. You may find this difficult at first, and the tendency will be to 'stab' at the ball. But if you practise you will find it works and assuming you have lined up carefully you will never be far off line. Many golfers would say that this particular technique is unorthodox, but one golfer who goes along with me on this point is Neil Coles, the Ryder Cup player. When practising, Neil puts down a coin about two inches in front of the ball, just out of the way of the line. Then he makes sure that the clubhead never follows-through past the coin.

On one point we all agree: **throughout the putt the head must be kept perfectly still, and this is the most essential aspect of every golf shot.** The great Irishman Harry Bradshaw, on his day a really great putter, used to say that he never looked up until he heard the ball rattle in the hole!

I deal now with the important ritual that must be carried out before every putt is taken—reading the green.

If you watch professionals playing a big tournament, you will notice how carefully they study the line of the putt. Before addressing the ball, they walk slowly to the hole, examining the texture of the grass. Then they decide the track of the putt by squatting down on their haunches, first behind the ball, then behind the hole, looking for subtle 'borrows' and slopes. They move all obstructions, even dead flies and whisps of grass, from the intended path of the ball. When they are quite satisfied that everything is right and they have the information they need, they address the putt and settle down in a relaxed manner.

There are two reasons why they go to such infinite care: to collect data, and to get rid of tension. When a putt is worth five hundred pounds you need all the information you can get!

But the other reason is almost as vital. Sensible professionals will not putt until they are one hundred per cent relaxed. Studying the putt not only tells what you want to know, it also gives you time to relax the body and get yourself into the right frame of mind. Weekend golfers often cannot (or do not) take quite so long over a putt. Folk playing behind are hard on your heels, and you are likely to become unpopular if you linger too long on the green! Nevertheless, try and be perfectly relaxed when you putt. You must 'feel' the putt, and you cannot do that if body-muscles are still tuned to the effort of hitting a long drive, or if you are still suffering the anguish of slicing your ball out of bounds.

In this most important aspect of 'low-scoring golf', it may be helpful if we examine what you should be looking for when you study the green. Well, you can start 'reading' the green long before you arrive. From a distance, you can see the general slopes of the putting surface in relation to the surrounding ground. Therefore, as soon as you have played your approach shot, make a habit of having a good look at the lie of the land as you walk towards the green. When you get there to take your first putt of, let's say, fifteen or twenty feet, study the texture and 'cut' of the grass. If the green has just been cut it will be 'fast' so you must not rap the ball too hard. Is the grain of the grass against you? If so, you must strike the putt a shade harder. If the ground slopes across your line, aim the putt on the top side of the hole. If the green is wet, then your putt must be stronger. These are the obvious things to watch for, and it is a good habit to register them automatically. None are unimportant, and for that reason I am setting down what you may decide are simple, common-sense dictums. I think maybe when you see these items in print they will register better.

Having a clear idea of the direction in which you want to hit the ball, try not to change your mind at the last moment. Above all, if you are going to miss the hole, make certain that you miss it on the far side—**don't be short**.

Try and be confident. If you miss a short putt, don't let it haunt you for the rest of the game. Dismiss it, and remember that holing one twenty-footer makes up for the yarder you missed.

Here and there you may find a 'natural' who is prone to hole long putts, like some folk are to have accidents. But they are few and far between. For you and me it is practice, practice, and more practice. One day you might discover the secret. If you do, tell me—we'll make a fortune together!

12

RECOVERING FROM SAND

THE main thing about any bunker: **Don't let it frighten you! The more you fear bunkers, the greater the chance of being trapped, and the more trouble you will have recovering.**

Hazards are categorised: fairway-bunkers, and those guarding the greens. They require different shots.

Bunkers can be deep, or shallow-faced; if they contain sand it may be soft or firm. If the bunker is shallow-faced and the sand is firm, there is no problem, providing the ball is 'sitting up' nicely. You can play the shot almost as you would any comparable distance iron-shot. But it is wise to take one or two clubs less (with more loft) than you would from the fairway. Also, wind up slower because the temptation is to hit from the top, and this usually means taking too much sand. If you keep your head down, and still, you should produce a good clean shot.

When the sand is soft, or the face of the bunker is deep, the main objective must always be to get out. This may sound elementary, but so many players imagine that hitting hard will get them far enough to make up for being in the trap.

When the ball lands in this kind of bunker, resign yourself to losing a stroke, and perhaps making it up by holing a long putt. If you take a club for length, the chances are that you will hit the top half of the ball and it will bury even deeper into the soft face of the bunker.

For playing from soft sand: Take a well-lofted iron and stand so that the ball is equi-distant from the feet. Make sure that your feet are firmly planted in the sand; move them about to get well 'dug in'. Without letting the sole of the club touch the sand —**it is against the rules to 'ground' the club at the address for a bunker-shot**—fix your eye on a spot about three inches behind the ball. That must be the point of entry of the clubhead into the sand on the downswing. Take the club back, slowly as usual, well inside the line by keeping your right elbow in; keep both feet firmly in the sand. If you raise your left heel as for other shots, your foot may slip and put the whole of your body out of correct alignment; besides, you are not after a full hip pivot, so 'foot-giving' is unnecessary. But take the club back as far as you can with a full shoulder turn, then hit—with power in your hands—that spot behind the ball. Strike right through the sand; don't quit, or 'break' the left wrist when the clubhead makes contact. The clubhead will actually travel right under the ball, and that is what we are after. If you play this shot correctly, the ball will go high in the air, well clear of the face of the bunker. Make sure that, although your hips scarcely move because you do not raise your left heel, plenty of clubhead speed is generated with your arms and hands. Don't be afraid of hitting hard—but be sure that the strike is made at least two inches (possibly more, if the sand is very soft) behind the ball.

It is important that your feet remain firmly 'dug in' throughout the shot from sand, and the knees should be slightly bent to keep the frame relaxed. Don't raise your head to see whether you are safely out of the bunker. If you do, you won't be!

This 'explosion' shot is also used when in soft sand around the green. Again, with complete shoulder-pivot, you should carry out a full arms-and-hands swing. This is really one of the easy shots in golf, once you have the trick, but beginners sometimes are reluctant to make the full hit when only a few feet from the green for fear of going over the back. The shot calls for courage, but often it can be a life-saver. Remember to **'explode' out by hitting the sand well behind the ball; the shorter the shot, the further behind the ball.** Follow-through, and the ball (with plenty of sand) will jump merrily from the trap.

G.—5

Bobby Locke, who was very good at these, called them 'splash' shots. It is an apt description, for hitting soft sand is almost like splashing through water. The clubhead must go right under the ball and come through the other side in one complete movement. Keep your head down until well after you have hit through. Let your right shoulder ride under your chin before you look up.

A final word: Don't be defeatist about bunkers. If you play a good bunker-shot nothing is more likely to give a jolt to your opponent's morale.

- PLAY THE BALL OFF THE LEFT FOOT.

- THE OPEN CLUBFACE STRIKES THE SAND WELL BEHIND THE BALL, THEN GOES THROUGH WITH A 'CHOP-ITS-LEGS-OFF' ACTION.

- IN THIS SHOT THERE IS VERY LITTLE BODY MOVEMENT. HANDS & ARMS DO MOST OF THE WORK.

The 'Splash' shot from SAND.

13

COPING WITH NATURAL HAZARDS

Bunkers are man-made, but in any round of golf Mother Nature provides plenty of her own kind of troubles. Some of these are just you, in the form of tensions, inhibitions, or plain carelessness. Then, there is the other kind of physical trouble made by nature. On the course these are called natural hazards.

Natural hazards vary from course to course. For example, a seaside links with fast sandy fairways and greens and a constant sea-breeze, will be a very different proposition to what you would expect on an inland, park-type course where the sub-soil is heavy clay. But no matter on what kind of course you play, you are bound to be faced with several common hazards.

Assuming you have progressed and to some extent have mastered the mechanics of the straightforward golf swing, 'muscle-memory' is becoming established and gradually you are getting what we called 'grooved'. I am going to describe four types of shots which are refinements, and which will help you under particular circumstances.

Hooking and slicing—intentionally

We have accepted the 'square' stance, in which the feet are parallel with the intended line of ball flight. If the feet are 'square', then the shoulders will be 'square' also; this means that you can get into the correct 'in to out' position in the hitting area. When properly struck, the flight of the ball will be slightly right to left, but the result gets you on target.

Let us suppose there is a clump of trees between you and the green. Hitting the ball straight would invite disaster. In this case, you contrive an alternate line of flight. Either you hook the ball around the trees from right to left, or you slice it round from left to right—whichever way looks easiest and safest.

If you decide **to hook your shot, you must close your stance**. The feet remain the same distance apart but the right foot is placed back a few inches. The position of the shoulders fall into line with your feet. Now, when you take the club back (as you have been taught) you will automatically increase the 'in to out' line. The result is that the shot 'hooks'—starting off to the right then bending quite violently to the left—and around the trees, if you have judged the bend correctly. The further back you place your right foot (and right shoulder) the more pronounced will be the hook.

To slice the shot from left to right you set up your stance in reverse by bringing the right foot forward. This 'opens' your shoulders so that they point well left of the target. Then, when you take the club back, the clubhead will go 'outside' and slice across the ball making it 'fade' from left to right.

Before you attempt the slice and the hook, practice is essential. Don't forget: **these shots are simply variations on the correct swing. Make certain that you can hit crisply and well using the orthodox 'square' stance before you experiment with the 'open' and 'closed' stance.**

Uphill and downhill shots

Few golf courses are entirely flat. During a round of golf you will be faced with shots to be played from the side of hills or slopes. The most difficult are from downhill lies.

Let us examine this particular natural hazard. First of all, it is important not to lean with the slope. To counteract this tendency, bend your right knee until the body is correctly aligned. Your feet should be fairly wide apart, making a firm, broad base so that you retain balance on the backswing.

When taking the club back, you will find that the slope tends to make your backswing too upright. This will mean that your right elbow may stray from the important 'tucked in' position; if the slope is really steep, it will be difficult to stay 'inside' the line. If you don't, the shot will probably slice, so make allowance by aiming to the left. Also, it is often a good idea to take a more lofted club than you would ordinarily use. This will help you to hit the ball fair and square.

For uphill lies, get the correct body-alignment by bending the left knee, and aim slightly to the right to counteract an almost inevitable hook. Also, take a club with less loft in the face, because the tendency is to hit the ball too high and short of the target.

When your feet at the address are either above or below the ball, you have yet another type of problem. If you are too far above the ball, try to 'sit back' on your heels to prevent losing balance during the swing. Grip the shaft lower down than usual; don't reach for the ball. There will be a tendency to slice, so emphasise the 'in to out' movement.

When you are below the ball, stand 'forward' on the feet. The 'in to out' movement will be exaggerated, so allow for a hook by aiming right of the target.

Playing shots from the rough

All courses have jungle country—areas which never see the greenkeeper's mower. As with bunker-shots, the first 'must' when playing from savage rough is to get out.

Often the rough is kindly short, and sometimes the ball sits up invitingly for you to have a go with a four-wood or three-iron. But always proceed with caution; check that the grass is not too lush, or a shallow-faced club might go under the ball without making a good impact. Wind up particularly slowly; don't raise your left heel; and keep your eye on the ball just that little bit longer.

If you are in a really tough spot, forget distance and concentrate on getting the ball on to the fairway. Take a deep-faced club—a seven- or nine-iron—and hold it well down the shaft. Then, with your feet wide apart for good anchorage, hit as hard as you can from 'in to out', keeping your head well down. Again, don't stab at the ball, but hit right through with your hands. As with bunkers there will be a tendency to quit at moment of impact. This will be disastrous, particularly in very deep rough, and you may bury the ball even deeper into the jungle. **Be bold, and hit hard with the hands.**

Into the wind

Here is a tip to remember: A good shot will hardly ever be affected by wind. So when you are playing in a howling gale (this can be fun) just keep swinging the club in the correct way, and you won't go far wrong. Don't try to beat the wind by hitting harder. This will merely upset that nice smooth arc, and you will start hitting jerkily from the top of the swing—instead of encouraging the club to gradually gather momentum so that the clubhead is swinging fastest when it makes contact with the ball. Remember to keep a firm, steady stance, and for this you should have your feet a little wider apart than usual.

There's nothing so satisfying as driving with a following wind. Tee the ball up nice and high (some take a two-wood in preference to a driver), this will get the ball high in the air where it will be helped by the wind and give extra length.

When the wind is against, tee the ball lower and your low trajectory shot will penetrate the oncoming wind.

Professionals and low-handicap amateurs, when playing in the wind, use the slice and hook shots to suit their convenience. For you, safety first. Although the wind does not 'bend' a good straight shot, it greatly exaggerates a hook or slice.

14

BOGEYS, BIRDIES, AND
FORMS OF PLAY

HAVING grasped the fundamentals of the golf swing, your style should progress naturally and easily, and soon you will be ready to graduate from the practice-ground to the battlefield. If all has gone well you will be anxious to get on to the course for your first round of golf. Before you arrange this step forward, read the following chapters. They are mainly about the game itself. If you assimilate the background, ethics and atmosphere, your appetite will be whetted for maximum fun and efficiency.

The object, of course, is to get the ball into the eighteen holes in as few shots as possible. As in all things, there are some folk who can do this better than others—for this reason there is a system of handicapping which enables players of varying standards to compete on equal terms. I'll explain the system. There is nothing like it in any other sport.

You can give a runner twenty-five yards start in a sprint, but this will only confirm what you already know—that you can run faster than he can. In snooker, you can give your opponent a start of two blacks, but again you are only proving that you are the better snooker-player. In fact, this applies in most games and sports where two players compete; only one, the better player, is handicapped. Not so in golf. The big difference between golf and any other game is that **both players are handicapped— the man who can play nearest to his own handicap wins**

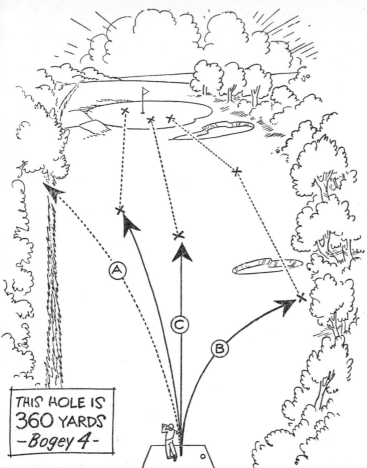

THIS HOLE IS
360 YARDS
—Bogey 4—

'A' ATTEMPTS A 'LONG ONE'— HE DRIVES OVER 200 yards, BUT HE HOOKS OUT OF BOUNDS—HIS FORFEIT MEANS THAT HIS UNDER SHOT IS FROM THE TEE — HE HOLES OUT FOR 6.

'B' SLICES TO A BAD POSITION—HE TAKES TWO MORE SHOTS TO AVOID BUNKERS—FINALLY, HE HOLES OUT FOR 5.

'C' TAKES IT EASY WITH A 190 YARD DRIVE—A COMFORTABLE 3-IRON SHOT LANDS ON THE GREEN — RESULT: BOGEY 4.

at golf. You are really playing against two opponents—the other fellow, and the course. If he's on his game, the other chap may be better able to master the course from his handicap than you can from yours—even although you are considered the better golfer.

How does the system work, and how should you set about getting a handicap?

Every golf course has what we call a Standard Scratch Score. This is the score in which a first-class golfer is expected to play the eighteen-hole circuit in ideal summer conditions. In the case of a nine-hole course, it represents two rounds.

The S.S.S. is fixed according to the length of the course, and this is the basic figure on which all handicaps at that club are determined. If a course is 6000 yards long, the S.S.S. will be in the region of 68, or perhaps a stroke or two more if it is set on difficult terrain. The average course has an S.S.S. of 70 or thereabouts. If you take ninety strokes for the round, on a course with an S.S.S. of 70 you will have played to a handicap of 20 (90 less 20 equals the S.S.S.). A scratch golfer has a handicap of 0. He should go round that same course in 70 strokes. In other words, to play to his handicap he must not drop a single shot. To achieve a handicap of, say, 16, you must be able to go round consistently in 86 strokes (86 less 16 equals S.S.S.). It is the nett score which counts.

When you play a round of golf, especially during these early days of your golfing career, always jot your score down, thus keeping an accurate record of your progress. A good idea is also to jot the number of putts you take, as well as other shots. This will show up weaknesses, and you will soon know which aspects of your game require most attention on the practice-ground. When you can consistently break the 'one-hundred barrier', you are all set to establish your first handicap. This is how it is done. On three separate rounds, ask fellow-members to record your totals on three score-cards. Hand these to the Secretary of the Club, and in turn they will be examined by the Handicapping Committee who use the average of your cards as a basis, then allot you a handicap which is duly established on the club notice-board. For example, if you submit rounds of 95, 94 and 93 on a course where the S.S.S. is 70, then you will be assessed a 24 handicap (this is the maximum for men; for women, it is 36).

When you have your first handicap, the next target is to get out of the twenties. Don't be content to stay too long on the same handicap; aim at improving your game constantly.

Score-cards are provided free by every golf club and contain a wealth of valuable information. Always carry one in your hip pocket and refer to it throughout the round. On it you will find the exact length of every hole. In time you will memorise the distances of your 'home' course and know which club to use for visibility circumstances which are often difficult.

Also on the score-card you will find that 'bogeys' are shown for each hole.

Bogey, like S.S.S., is assessed by length. Generally speaking, they are decided as follows: 250 yards and under is bogey three—in other words, the first-class player is expected to drive on to the green, then he is allowed two putts. Holes of between 251 and 475 yards are bogey four (on for two; two putts), holes of over 475 yards are bogey five (on for three; two putts). Remember, these bogeys represent the scores of first-class players. It seldom works out that anyone gets eighteen successive bogeys; usually odd shots are dropped on certain holes and picked up on others.

The total of the eighteen bogeys represents the bogey for the course; this is usually called the 'par'.

One of the advantages of golf is that you don't have to play against an opponent. It is preferable, of course, but if you are alone you can still have plenty of fun playing against bogey. On the score-card you will find another column of figures which is called the 'stroke index', and this is how it works:

When you are playing against someone who has a lower handicap than yourself, he must give you three-quarters of the difference between your handicaps. Suppose you are playing from 24, against a man whose handicap is 12; subtract his handicap from yours, this leaves 12, and three-quarters means 9. On every hole where the stroke-index shows 8 or under, you receive a one-stroke allowance. So if you both take five shots on this hole, you win, because after deducting your handicap allowance shot your tally is nett four.

In match-play, the player winning most holes is the victor. When playing alone against bogey, the stroke-index works the same way. Simply take three-quarters of your handicap and 'receive' one shot on each hole indicated. The result shows you to be either 'up' or 'down' on bogey.

There are many forms of competitive golf. You can play against one opponent, or a hundred simultaneously, if you are involved in 'stroke' play (as opposed to 'match' play).

You can play in pairs (fourball), each golfer playing with his own ball for the side, or you can play 'foursomes', in which each pair plays with one ball which is struck alternately. So the formula is: **match-play**—when the object is to win as many holes as possible; **stroke-play**—when the total number of shots for the round (less handicap) counts.

In a **Bogey Competition** any number of players (going out in pairs) compete against the 'card' of the course. **Stableford** is an attractive form of play. You use a system of points-scoring: one point for a hole achieved in a nett score of one-over bogey, two points for a bogey, three points for a 'birdie' (i.e. one under bogey), and so on.

In all these forms of golf the game is fundamentally the same, but tactics vary, and later I propose to deal with the mental side which plays an important role in golf. The right psychological approach is often the difference between winning and losing.

First, however, you must know the rules.

15

GETTING TO KNOW THE RULES

LIKE legal documents, the rules of any game make heavy reading. Golf is no exception. Nevertheless, the main regulations should be studied carefully during these early days. Knowledge of them will greatly increase your general understanding of the game. Also, you will be able to devote one hundred per cent of your attention to the complex business of getting the ball into the hole —without having to worry about procedure.

The Rules of Golf cover every conceivable incident likely to arise, and each one is important. But for the time being, I am selecting fifteen which positively you must register. When you have learned these thoroughly, you are adequately equipped to cope with all normal situations. Of course, for more comprehensive details the Rule Book must be consulted. The undermentioned, however, will help you to hold your own in most locker-room arguments.

Fourteen clubs—maximum

Even before you leave the clubhouse, always check to see that you are not carrying more than fourteen clubs. This can happen when you have a matched set, plus a couple of alternative putters. Get into the habit of carrying out this check before every round —the penalties are severe in competitive golf: Match-play— loss of one hole for each excess club (maximum penalty is two holes per club); Stroke-play—two strokes for each excess club (maximum is four strokes per club).

The 'Honour'

When you reach the first tee, toss a coin to decide which player is going to drive off first. This is the best way, but sometimes it is a prerogative which goes to the player with the lowest handicap. Thereafter, the winner of the previous hole takes the 'honour'. No penalties for breaking this rule—but your opponent, in match-play, is entitled to ask you to re-drive if you have played out of turn.

Playing out of turn

Always it is the ball farthest from the hole which must be played first. Again, no penalty for a breach of the rule, but your opponent may ask you to re-play if you are at fault.

Advice

This one is regularly broken by weekend golfers: You must not ask for advice from your opponent. This means that you may not ask him which club he used for any particular stroke. Mostly this infringement occurs on short holes when a player is undecided as to which iron to use from the tee.

Lost ball

Five minutes is the maximum searching-time allowed to find a lost ball. After that, return to the original spot from which the ball was played and have another go—adding a penalty stroke.

Unplayable lie

If you have driven into a hopeless position from which it is impossible to strike the ball—say, in the middle of a gorse bush —you may do one of two things: either, drop the ball within two club-lengths of the unplayable spot (not nearer the hole) and add two penalty strokes, or, if you prefer, return to the original spot and play another ball, adding one penalty stroke. You, as the striker, are the sole judge as to whether your ball is unplayable anywhere on the course.

Out of bounds

Your score-card will indicate which places are out of bounds, and where the boundaries are. If you have hit your ball out of

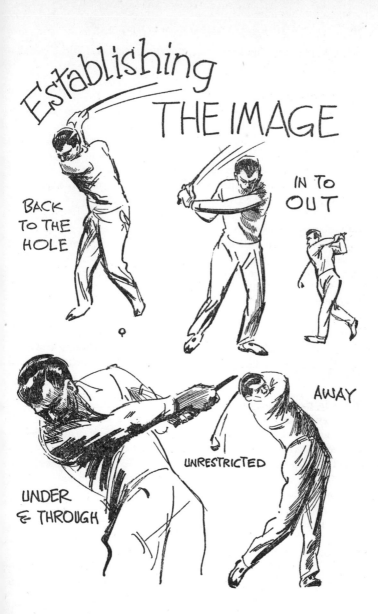

Establishing
THE IMAGE

BACK
TO THE
HOLE

IN TO
OUT

UNDER
& THROUGH

UNRESTRICTED

AWAY

bounds, play another shot from the same spot and add a penalty stroke.

Improving the lie

Never do anything which improves the lie of your ball. You must not bend or break anything which is growing—except to take your normal stance, or in the execution of the actual shot. Watch tournament professionals playing shots from deep trouble. Often they take several minutes to decide how to play them, so that they do not infringe. Penalties: match-play—loss of hole; stroke-play—two strokes.

Loose impediments

Except in hazards, you can move stones or wisps of dead grass from around your ball before you take a shot. But beware that you do not cause the ball to move—penalty: one stroke.

Hazards

Two things to watch for when you are in a sand-bunker, or a water hazard: you must not move anything from around the ball, nor touch the ground with your club before making a stroke. Penalties: match-play—loss of hole; stroke-play—add two strokes.

Playing the wrong ball

Always identify your ball before making a stroke (on the first tee it is a good idea to check that your opponent is not playing with a ball with similar identification-marks). In match-play, you lose the hole if you are the first to strike the wrong ball. In stroke-play, two strokes must be added—then you should play the correct ball. Hazards are an exception: if you play the wrong ball from a bunker there is no penalty, providing you rectify the error immediately.

'Rub of the green'

If your ball hits an 'outside agency'—that is to say, something or someone who is not taking part in your game—this is known as 'rub of the green'. There is no penalty, and the ball is played from where it lies. But anyone taking part in the game, including a caddie, is not an 'outside agency'. In match-play, if your ball is deflected by your opponent, his caddie, or any of his equipment —**he loses the hole.** If it hits your caddie, or your equipment— **you lose the hole.** If stroke-play, two strokes must be added to the score of the offending side.

On the green

Before you putt you may repair pitch-marks, clean your ball (but mark it carefully and return it to the exact spot) and move any loose impediments from your putting 'line'. But don't test the putting surface by pressing down on it with either your putter or your hands. Penalties: match-play—loss of hole; stroke-play—two strokes.

To increase your chances of holing out, you may select either to leave the flagstick in the hole, remove it before you play, or have the flag attended by someone (who must then remove it as soon as you have struck the ball).

Practice

On the day of a stroke competition, do not practise on the course before you play your round. Take special care of this one —the penalty is usually disqualification, even for innocent chip-shots to while away the time.

Scoring

At the end of your round in a stroke-play competition, your card should be signed by the marker and countersigned by yourself. Make sure that all the facts are correct, for once the card has been submitted, no alterations can be made. Again, disqualification is the likely penalty.

I stress that these are merely a rough guide to help the beginner. The Rule Book must be consulted for the more unusual occurrences.

G.—6

16

'HE'S A NICE CHAP TO PLAY WITH'

IF you are thus described, you will never seek in vain for a game. This brief chapter contains all you need to know about the niceties of golf. They fall under two headings. First, there is 'considerations for your opponent'. In this connection, you should remember these points:

1. Never move, talk, or stand too close to a golfer when he is playing a shot. Remember, every golf shot needs maximum concentration. Give the player silence, and plenty of room. He will then probably reciprocate for you.

2. Don't get so absorbed in your own game that you completely ignore your opponent. Be charitable; give him credit for good shots, but keep a discreet silence when he plays badly. Don't criticise his swing unless asked. Maybe it took years of sweat and blood to develop.

3. Always give the impression that you are enjoying the game —even 'though playing badly. Try not to show ill-temper after a bad shot—there is nothing more embarrassing than to witness the ugly side of someone's nature. Don't forget, your opponent has his own worries.

4. Accept defeat graciously. Look cheerful when your opponent pockets your half-crown, remembering that, if you have observed these rules, you will always have a chance to win it back.

Secondly, remember these general rules of etiquette. They help to make the game run smoothly, and greatly add to the pleasure of all concerned.

1. Never play a stroke until you are absolutely certain that the players in front are out of range.

2. Don't delay. When you and your opponent have finished putting, replace the flag and move off the green. Don't stop to check your score-card until you are well away from where the players behind want their shots to land.

3. Never leave a bunker without first smoothing the sand. Few things are more annoying than having to play from someone else's heel-mark.

4. Always repair the marks made by pitch-shots on the greens. Replace all divots.

5. Let the players following you come through if you are searching for a lost ball, and do not continue to play until they are out of range.

6. If you are playing in a three- or four-ball game you must 'give way' to singles and foursomes. Also, let the players behind you come through if you lose more than one clear hole on the match in front. If the Captain of the Club is playing immediately behind, invite him through. This courtesy is always extended; likewise he takes preference and honour on the tee.

YOU MUST HAVE A CLEAR

MENTAL PICTURE

OF WHAT YOU ARE
TRYING TO DO
IN THE HITTING
AREA

RIGHT ELBOW IS
WELL TUCKED-IN
—
HEAD QUITE STILL
-AS AT ADDRESS
—
LEFT HAND AND
ARM UNDER FULL
CONTROL
—
WEIGHT IS ALMOST
ENTIRELY
TRANSFERRED
TO THE LEFT —
WHICH REMAINS
FIRM, AS BOTH
HIPS TURN
TO THE
LEFT

STANCE IS
TAKEN
WITH THE
BALL
EQUI-DISTANT
FROM
BOTH FEET.

IN TO OUT

A FULL SHOT WITH A 5-IRON ....

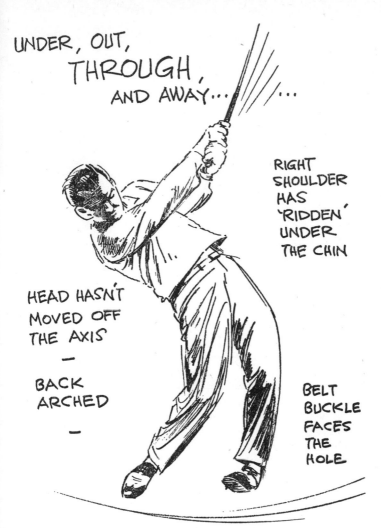

17

BEATING YOUR OPPONENT
IN MATCH-PLAY

THE thing about golf is that you have fun whether you win or lose. But competition is always the spice, and it is true to say that you get *more* fun if you go all out to win.

You have seen that there are basically two forms of competitive golf: **match-play**, in which you compete against one opponent hole by hole; and **stroke-play**, when it is the total number of strokes for the round that counts. Tactics vary, though the object of the game is the same—to get the ball into the hole using as few shots as possible.

One of the funniest passages I have read appeared in a book by Horace Hutchinson, written in 1886. Hutchinson was one of the great amateur golfers of his time, and this was the advice he gave to beginners on how to compete in match-play:

'If you find yourself being outplayed by the excellent iron approaches of your adversary, it is sometimes a good plan to say to him, in a tone of friendly interest: "Really you are playing wonderfully well today—better than I ever saw you play before. Can you account for it in any way?" This is likely to promote a slight nervousness when he next takes an iron in his hands; and this nervousness is likely, if the match is at all a close one, to be of considerable service to you. There is no rule to prevent your doing this; only, after a time, people will cease to play with you.'

I don't know what they called these tactics in 1886, but

nowadays they would come under the heading 'gamesmanship'. And as Mr. Hutchinson said, you will lose a good many friends that way! I do not recommend that approach, but there are other rules which you should observe.

Of course, I am playing this game for a living, and I am not going to suggest that you try to develop the same sort of big-match temperament that we professionals must cultivate. You are playing strictly for fun—for us it is bread and butter. Even so, your golf will improve beyond measure if you take every match seriously, and go all out to win.

Rule No. 1 in match-play golf is this: **Remember that you have two opponents—the other chap and the course. Concentrate on beating the course.**

Too many golfers get so wrapped up in what their opponent is doing that they fail to concentrate on their own golf. There will be a great tendency, particularly in the early days, to be awe-struck at the prospect of playing against a more experienced golfer. At first, you will probably try hitting the ball as far as he does from the tee. Resist this temptation at all costs; just play your own natural game and concentrate on scoring well. From handicap you stand just as much chance of winning as he does—more, in fact, for the bigger they are, the harder they fall. The fatal mistake is to try and match him, club for club. When, on a short hole, he takes a five-iron from the tee, do not be afraid to take your No. 3, if you think it necessary to get the distance.

When I compete in the Professional Match-Play Championship, I completely ignore my opponent and concentrate entirely on beating the course. Sometimes, in fact, I get so engrossed in my own play that I have to ask my caddie what is the state of the game. I know that if I am beating the course, the chances are that I am also beating my opponent. In other words, I prefer to make the other chap do the sweating! This, I am sure, is the secret of match-winning golf.

Rule No. 2: **Don't show your emotions.** No matter how disturbed you are at missing a three-foot putt, try not to show it. Once you display temperament, you put the initiative into your opponent's court. It's not always easy, but keep steady and 'poker-faced'. I was once playing Dave Thomas in the 'News of the World' Tournament, and in the early part of the round Dave was getting the better of things. Then, slowly I began to reduce the deficit. Dave kept mum—but when beads of sweat started to appear on his brow, I knew I almost had him. From being in an almost impossible position, I managed to square the match on the last green. Dave won on the twenty-second hole —but by showing me how worried he was, he had almost let me in. **When things are going wrong, keep your head.**

Rule No. 3: **The last putt of the match is no more difficult than the first—always play it boldly.** I learned this one at Ganton, in 1953, and I always try to put it into practice.

I was up against Dai Rees in the final of the 'Match-Play'. Dai had won the title no fewer than four times before.

He and I have the same approach to match-play. He likes to concentrate entirely on playing the course, and not his opponent, and he shows hardly any emotion during the round. We have been friends for years, but during that Final neither of us were in the mood for an old pal's act. I don't suppose we spoke more than half a dozen words throughout the thirty-six holes.

During the morning round I managed to build up a comfortable lead; at lunchtime I was four holes up. I was still four up with only nine holes to play—when things began to go wrong for me. Instead of pressing home my advantage, I began to let the match slip away. Also, Dai pulled out three wonderful birdies and squared the match on the 35th hole.

Everything hung on the last hole. Dai played a great drive; mine was hooked into a jungle of high trees on the left of the fairway. Dai pushed his second to the right of the green; I managed to recover well to finish just over the back of the green in semi-rough.

His chip stopped six yards short of the hole ;mine was eleven feet away. Dai putted: a great putt which for an agonising second looked like dropping. But it hung on the lip of the hole and refused to go down. Now it all rested on my eleven-footer. Holing it meant the winner's cheque of £750, and missing meant playing down the 37th hole—with the initiative firmly in Dai's grasp. I decided then what I am advising now. I had to putt boldly as though this was the first, not the last putt of the round. Without wasting much time, I struck the ball firmly. It moved along like a child running to its mother, hit the back of the hole, then rattled in.

If you observe these three rules, you will never be easy to beat. And if you do lose, your opponent will have earned his half-crown the hard way!

18

THE WAY TO LOW SCORING

THERE is one aspect of this game which I have studied and practised more than most. I am referring to the recovery-shot. Any success I have had on the tournament circuit is largely due to the fact that, for me, 'trouble' on a golf course holds no terrors.

As a youngster at Bramley—where my father was Professional and, incidentally, holds the professional course record with a 63 —I spent hours playing 'trick' shots from the most impossible positions. For me, the 'trouble' shot was not only challenging, but it also intrigued me and offered a special brand of fun and interest which, maybe, is common to my particular mental make-up.

Now I am firmly convinced that **intelligent recovery-shots —and sound putting—are the complete answers to low scoring in stroke-play competition.**

There is one big difference between match- and stroke-play. In match-play, you always have another chance. One bad hole does not necessarily mean defeat. If you find yourself in deep trouble, there is no need to despair; you may redeem the situation by winning the next hole. Not so in stroke-play, when every shot counts. The tension is on from the first drive to the final putt, and you must not relax for a moment. One loose shot can destroy your chances of winning—if you don't know how to set about getting out of trouble.

As I say, right at the start of my playing career I concentrated mostly on recovery-shots. At least half of every practice-session was devoted to playing from bunkers, gorse bushes, long grass, and chipping over trees. In time I was playing these trouble-shots with neither effort nor anxiety. I believe it has paid handsome dividends.

I am not suggesting, of course, that to win medal competitions you must be able to recover like a professional. But I do advise the beginner to devote plenty of time to the more unusual type of shots so that he learns to play them without worry. In stroke-play, one bad shot can throw you out; make you lose rhythm. If you can get into the right frame of mind when you are in deep rough, I believe you will have won half the battle. Be prepared to forfeit a stroke, if necessary, by making sure that you get out. Too many golfers make things worse by attempting miracle-shots, when safety-play is best.

The most satisfactory shot I have ever played was a recovery, though I admit there was an element of risk involved, which I would not advise a beginner to take. However, when I have described what took place I think you will appreciate the thrill I had when it came off. In any case, it reflected my past training and serves to make the point that practice, practice, and more practice is the only way.

The shot was played at Portrush, in 1951, and undoubtedly it helped me to become the British Open Champion.

I had been playing well all week, and after three rounds had built up a comfortable lead of six strokes on the field. But at the 16th hole in the final round, I almost ruined my chance. From the tee my drive was badly hooked; the ball hit a five-stepped stile well to the left of the fairway. The stile had prevented my ball going out of bounds, and I was thanking my lucky stars—until we reached the spot, and I surveyed the frightful position from which I had to play my second shot. The ball was lying so close to a barbed-wire fence that I had to adopt a sideways stance to prevent lacerating the backs of my hands on the wire. This story could have been the tragedy of my life!—instead it is a joy to tell. I thought over the problem and decided that the best way to strike the ball was to attempt a most uncomfortable slice.

The shot came off beautifully; the ball soared high, curled sharply in mid-air, dropped like a skylark, and pitched by the flag. What could have been a disastrous six was turned into a highly satisfactory four. Frank Stranahan, the great American who had won the British Amateur Championship the previous year, was playing with me. He watched the shot from the other side of the fairway, then walked fully fifty yards towards me with his hand outstretched.

'Max,' he said, 'that's the greatest shot I ever saw in my life.'

The compliment was all the more welcome, as those were the first words Frank had spoken to me all day—we had formed a pact not to speak to each other during the final two rounds.

I didn't really appreciate the value of that recovery-shot until later in the afternoon. Out among the mighty sand-dunes, a few holes behind, the swarthy little Argentinian Antonio Cerda, was reeling off great figures. The news had reached us in the club-house that Cerda was still very much in the hunt. It was even beginning to look as though he might snatch victory, or at least tie for first place. I admit I was worried at the time by the prospect of a play-off for the title; everything I had was put into the four rounds of the Championship, and I considered my energy, both physical and mental, was about spent.

When Cerda reached the dramatic sixteenth, he needed to finish with three fours to tie. Strangely enough, from that same tee where I had pulled my drive, Antonio played an almost identical shot! In fact, his hook finished as close to the wire fence as mine had about an hour earlier. Poor Cerda! Perhaps he had not done his homework. Anyway, he fluffed his second shot, took a disastrous six, and the Championship was mine.

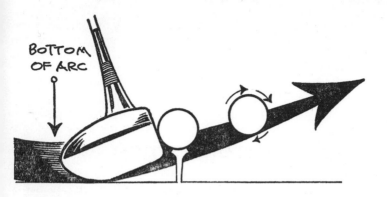

BOTTOM OF ARC

THE DRIVE, WITH THE CLUBHEAD RISING TO STRIKE THE TEED-UP BALL, THUS IMPARTING TOP-SPIN WHICH MAKES THE BALL 'RUN' WHEN LANDING ON FAIRWAY.

IRON SHOT, WITH THE BALL 'SQUEEZED' AGAINST THE GROUND AS THE ANGLED CLUBHEAD BITES INTO THE BALL IMPARTING BACK-SPIN FOR 'STOP' AND ACCURACY.

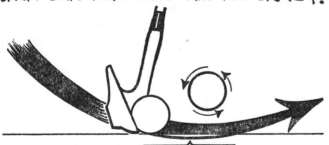

DIVOT SCAR
BOTTOM
OF ARC

19

YOUR COMPETITION DAY

WHEN you have established a handicap you will be eligible to play in Club Competitions. Later, it is to be hoped that your game will go from strength to strength, and perhaps you may qualify to play in more senior events like Open Meetings, County Alliances, and so on. It is essential, during these early days, that you develop the right temperament for competitive golf. Nothing is so frustrating as having the ability, but lacking the correct mental approach.

Competitive golf is great fun—but it needs a tidy, methodical mind, and cool nerve. Everything must be right if you are to pick up some trophies. From the moment you get up on the morning of a competition, almost everything you do has some bearing on your performance in the match. Holes in your socks, a domestic quarrel, a careless snick with your razor—little things like these can add strokes to your score. I am an old campaigner with thirty years of nerve-racking, cash-golf behind me, so believe me, I know. Golf is the most sensitive mechanism. Tranquility must be there, if you are to have the rhythm needed for good shot-making.

Watch these things on your Big Day. They may help to make it bigger.

You must 'feel' right

Long before you arrive at the course, try and develop a sense of rhythm in everything you do. Give yourself plenty of time; don't rush things.

I like to have everything ready the evening before a tournament; clean, polished clubs, trousers nicely pressed, and shoes so brightly polished that I lead the field in this respect from the word 'go'. When I reach the clubhouse, I give myself plenty of time to change, because I know that if I have to hurry on to the first tee, rhythm will go, and it may well take several holes before I settle down.

To feel right, I like to be dressed right. I reckon that if a man is untidy on a golf course, his game will also be untidy. To be frank, I would never put my money on a man who plays in dirty shoes, or who tucks his trousers into his socks. Take my tip: always wear good clothes for golf. You start off with a certain superiority that is good for you and bad for your opponent.

People are constantly referring to my golf-dress. 'Clown Prince of Golf', I have been called, or 'Max, the Playboy'. Well, it's true that I like wearing rather colourful clothes. Gay clothes do not suit everyone—although I don't believe anyone should look drab on a golf course—but for me they are fine. A tournament golfer should remember that, as an entertainer, he has a certain duty to the spectator-public. There are many ways of giving good value to the spectators, and a 'different brand image' helps.

But the main reason why I am clothes-conscious is this: **When I am well-dressed I have a comfortable feeling of well-being and confidence. This often reflects itself in the way I hit the ball!**

Relax

Complete relaxation during a competition is difficult, but important. The moment you 'tense up', muscles restrict and your natural swing stiffens into a series of jerks. We all have our 'tricks' which help us to relax.

Irishman Fred Daly used to whistle softly to himself between shots; Sam Snead chats to his golf ball! I sometimes talk with spectators to relieve the tension; others prefer never to speak, but chew gum the whole way round. Eric Brown (and too many others, including myself!) finds cigarette smoking helps, and is rarely seen without one during a tournament. Arnold Palmer is a chain-smoker, and when he tried to stop his game went off.

Whatever the mannerism, the object is to keep as relaxed as possible—even when things are going wrong.

No golfer can honestly say that he doesn't suffer from competition nerves. **The really clever, disciplined chap never shows his nerves. Any indication that you are 'worried' is a tremendous fillip to your opponent.**

When you watch tournament professionals, you will probably think they have nerves of iron. Mostly, they are as nervous as kittens—but they have learned the secret of control.

Walk around with the top golfers. Observe how ice-cool they appear to be. You get an idea how they really feel when they slot the winning putt. The disciplined control breaks, and even the dour ones have been known to fling their club aside and do a jig!

Concentrate

This is an absolute 'must'—all the time. As you walk between shots, decide on how you will play the next. Be clear in your mind about what you want to achieve, but having decided, don't change ideas.

Forget 'the other fellow' entirely. Concentrate on your own game and simply try to play within your handicap. Do that, and you'll win more often than not.

20

CLINIC

WHEN a man is ill he should go and see his doctor. It is the same with a golfer. If there is something persistently wrong with his golf he should seek professional attention. When a man merely has a headache or a common cold, he can usually get relief from aspirin or cough-sweets. Likewise, when a golfer suffers only from a slight tendency to slice or hook his shots, he should first try to make the necessary adjustments himself. With most minor complaints, an hour on the practice-ground usually does the trick—if the golfer knows what to look for. If the faults persist, he should consult his professional.

Often, a golf-fault creeps in without you noticing. The common cause of the hook, for example, is holding the club with the right hand too far under the shaft. That position, although incorrect, by usage can feel comfortable. In time, the hand gets so far under that it actually becomes uncomfortable to hold the club in the correct way. So, as soon as you develop a bad habit, take immediate steps to put it right before you get 'grooved' the wrong way. **You must not attempt to live with an incorrect golf swing. Change before it gets comfortable.**

When you know what causes a bad shot, you are halfway to knowing how to put it right. In this chapter I am going to deal with the six most common faults in golf, their causes, and how to cure them. Please check up on these points when things go wrong (which, from time to time, happens to the best of us).

SLICING

Usual cause: Striking the ball from 'out to in'.

Result: Ball curves viciously from left to right, and loses distance.

Without a doubt, this is the most common fault in golf—particularly with beginners.

I take you back to our wedge-under-the-door demonstration in Chapter 1. If the thick end is struck by the mallet coming across, 'out to in', the thin end of the wedge will be pushed to the right—and this is exactly what happens to the golf ball when it is struck with a similar action. **Right from the start of the backswing, the clubhead must be kept inside the line.**

There are a number of things to check.

First, the grip. Watch the position of your hands. The V's formed by the thumbs and forefingers of both hands should point to your right shoulder. If they are pointing to your left shoulder (which is usually the case with 'slicers') you are almost bound to take the clubhead outside the line on the backswing, and it will certainly strike the ball when moving down, 'out to in'. See at least two and a half knuckles on your left hand at the address. It will help to get the club in the correct position at the top of the backswing. Also, you will find it is easier to keep the right elbow comfortably in the correct 'tucked in' position.

Next, look at your feet. Are they 'square' (parallel) to the line of flight? If the line in front of your toes points left, this too may cause a slice. From that position, the clubhead is outside the line almost from the moment you take it away from the ball on the backswing.

Then, check your wind-up. Are you taking the clubhead away from the ground too soon? Remember, if you cock the wrists early this may aggravate the complaint. The clubhead should stay as close to the ground as possible for the first three feet of the backswing. This means moving the hands, arms and shoulders in one piece. Do not start cocking the wrists until they are about waist-high.

For quick reference, I will emphasise these points in black type, so if 'slicing' is your big headache, keep your book-marker in this page.

1. **Hands—V's point to your right shoulder.**
2. **Feet—'Square' to the line of flight.**
3. **Backswing—don't cock the wrists too soon; keep the clubhead close to the ground for the first yard; shoulders must turn until your back faces the hole.**

HOOKING

Usual cause: **Rolling the wrists on the downswing, and causing the club-face to 'shut'.**

Result: **Ball curves in flight smartly from right to left.**

A ball struck correctly will bend slightly in the air from right to left. This is called 'draw'. The hooked shot greatly exaggerates this bend. While the sliced ball loses length, the hook actually increases length because the ball has top-spin—which means that it can penetrate into even deeper trouble!

You might say that a hook is directly opposite to a slice. The hands are too far round the right-hand side of the club-shaft, and the feet are 'closed' (the line in front of the toes points too far right).

Again, the answer to your problem may be in the position of the hands. Can you see too many knuckles of your left hand, or is your right hand too far under the shaft? Don't forget I have said that golf is primarily a left-handed game. This is a point of disagreement among certain teachers. Most say the hands are equally important; some even urge that the right hand is the prime mover. But I stick to what I have always believed: educate and strengthen the left, and the right will come in when necessary.

When you grip the club too far under the shaft with the right, you are inviting it to roll the wrists in such a way that the face of the club closes, or hoods. This invariably hooks the shot to

the left and at worst 'smothers' the ball so that it scarcely
rises.

Make sure that your feet are not in a line which points too far
to the right of your target. This will mean that your shoulders,
too, point that way, and you will greatly over-emphasise the
'in to out' movement.

Watch these points if you are a 'hooker':

1. **V's of your grip must point to your right shoulder,
   but no further right than that.**
2. **Stance should be 'square' to the target. See that
   your right foot has not crept back.**
3. **Don't roll the wrists when going back.**
4. **Finish with the hands high to ensure that you have
   not 'shut' the club-face at impact.**

SHANKING

Usual cause: Hitting the ball from 'out to in' with the
club-face open. Often the ball is actually
struck with the angle where the shaft
joins the blade.

Result: The ball shoots off, sometimes nearly
ninety degrees, to the right of the intended
direction.

This is golf's mystery-shot. It plagues even the most
experienced golfers from time to time, and the results can be
catastrophic. Shanks are most likely to occur with short shots of
less than a hundred yards, and believe it or not, they often happen
because the player takes too much trouble. In being over-careful,
he sometimes **puts** the clubhead to the ball, instead of letting it
swing.

Curiously, shanking comes in spells. It is unlikely that you
will have just one in a round. Once you have suffered, the
chances are that you will be terribly aware, and in an effort to
control the shot, you may make matters worse, playing three or

The EXPLOSION *Bunker shot*

- TAKEN OFF THE FRONT FOOT.
- HIT THE SAND BEHIND THE BALL.
- KEEP HEAD DOWN AND STILL.
- WRISTS BREAK QUICKLY ON THE BACKSWING, THEN MAKE A FULL FOLLOW-THROUGH ————

The UNDER-TREE *Problem shot*

- OFF THE RIGHT FOOT.
- HANDS WELL AHEAD OF BALL AT ADDRESS.
- SHORTEN THE BACKSWING, KEEP CLUBFACE CLOSED • USE A 4-IRON.

four consecutively. But, as I say, knowing the cause is halfway to finding a cure.

Sometimes a shank occurs when you are playing good golf, which makes the shot even more baffling. The only thing to do is make a bee-line for the practice-ground immediately on finishing the round. Then, get **swinging** until you are back in your natural, flowing 'groove'. Make sure that you are taking the clubhead back inside, then hit through the ball with both hands. The main reason for shanking is that the player, although he may be swinging correctly with his arms, is not snapping his hands through. Consequently, the club-face is left wide open at impact, and the ball is struck with the 'shank' of the clubhead (or 'neck', where the clubhead joins the shaft).

If you are stricken by shanking, observe these points:

1. **Backswing—Make sure that you keep 'inside' the line.**
2. **Downswing—Hit with the hands, as well as the arms; this will prevent the club-face being too open at impact.**

TOPPING

Usual cause: **Raising the head, therefore the rest of the body, as you strike the ball.**

Result: **The ball is struck 'above the equator' and runs along the ground.**

Inexperienced golfers 'top' the ball because they are too anxious to see where it has gone after the strike. The backswing may be perfect, but you will not hit the ball cleanly into the air if you do not stay down long enough.

The moment you raise your head, you cause the shoulders to come up also. What you must do, therefore, is to keep your eyes fixed to the spot where the ball was until your right shoulder is well and truly under your chin.

For all shots, keep your head down until after impact.

SMOTHERING

Usual cause: Hooding the club-face at impact.

Result: The ball is sent along the ground, well to the left of the intended direction.

There is a great tendency in any instructional book to repeat. This is inevitable when the author is trying to impress upon the reader certain vital points. However, this time I am going to put my favourite phrase another way: **golf is not a right-handed game!** If you allow your right hand to play too important a part in the golf swing, one of the results is likely to be the 'smother'.

At the time of writing, I am training four young professionals to play top-class tournament golf, in the hope that at least one of them will become a Champion. In the course of their instruction each youngster is learning to hit a golf ball two hundred yards—**using only the left hand.** In my opinion each of these boys is a potential world-beater. They can all hit the ball three hundred yards with a normal swing—and that is how I rate the importance of the left hand in golf. **At least two-thirds of the power/ accuracy element in a golf swing comes from a strong, disciplined left hand.**

FLUFFING

Usual cause: Swaying the body and hitting without pausing at the top of the backswing.

Result: The clubhead hits the ground behind the ball.

The most important aspect of every golf shot from tee to hole, is a perfectly still head. It must not move one inch on its axis from the time you address the ball, until you have hit through and the right shoulder is under your chin. When you move your head, you also move your shoulders—and the whole of your body is out of alignment. This is often what happens when you fluff a shot. On the backswing there is a tendency to sway over to the right, then, on the downswing, you sway back again. Sometimes you may be lucky with timing, but mostly the clubhead will thud into the ground before it reaches the ball.

To hit the ball fair and square, the swing must be right. This means observing the subtle pause at the top. This, as I have mentioned, is one of the secrets of good timing.

If, then, you are consistently fluffing shots, remember:

1. **Keep your head still throughout the swing, then you won't sway going back.**
2. **Observe the pause at the top.**
3. **Maintain good balance by keeping the knees slightly bent for good anchorage.**

The best cure for the six faults I have mentioned is practice—the correct way. Make sure that you practise your worst shots. Too many golfers—even young professionals—prefer to practise the shots they like best. Admittedly it is more fun cracking good shots with your favourite club, but it does not help your game when you are out on the course. If you have a tendency to slice with a three-iron, then practise with that club until you have got that shot right.

'Keep at it'—that is the three-word formula which ensures good golf for anyone who has a grasp of the correct mechanism.

I have listed the six cardinal faults in golf. There is something else. Most players—and it is not always to do with age—sometimes 'lose length from the tee'. You are hitting the ball sweetly enough, it goes straight without slice or hook. Yet the ball is not going as far as formerly. There are two things you can do and both will work to advantage.

To begin with, see that your shoulders have not got lazy. **They must make maximum turn.** If you are over forty-five, don't attempt the 'twist turn' with the left shoulder very low. This is for the lissom youngsters—even then it can cause slipped discs! Try the full pivot with your left shoulder only slightly lower than the right at the top of the backswing—the clubhead will still reach the correct position, if you keep the right elbow in.

The other essential for real length is strong, operative hands. Exercise from the elbows down to the fingertips; particularly the left. I go along with Henry Cotton in the belief that good hands, and a still head, can make a very fair golf shot—no matter what else happens.

21

DOING YOUR HOMEWORK

No golfer reaches the heights without strong hands and fore-arms; if also he has good muscles in his legs and back, so much the better. Hands are No. 1 priority because they take consider-able strain of keeping the clubhead square to the ball during ball-resistance at impact.

On demobilisation from the Royal Air Force at the end of the war I was in pretty good shape because I had done duty as a physical-culture instructor. Unfortunately, my golf muscles had been out of use for too long, so the first thing I had to do, if I was to achieve my ambition to be a top tournament golfer, was to get things in order. Almost by accident I discovered that the best way to increase tendon elasticity and strengthen fingers and wrists is to milk cows!

This little trick of mine has been written-up a dozen times by reporters and possibly many golfers have adopted this method. There is, of course, the obvious difficulty of procuring a cow! So we devise more orthodox methods. One of them is with the tennis ball. You simply squeeze it whenever you are sitting in front of the television, or reading a book. Just squeeze with all fingers, but twice as much work with the left hand, please. If you are a normal right-handed player, the left must always take command. It must control the arc and must never be over-powered by the right hand.

There is the amusing and popular hand-pressing game which is splendid for the wrists and forearms. Two players sit facing.

With elbows firm on the table, the opponents clasp hands and push until one is overcome and has his hand pressed back on to the table. Another is the excellent 'praying' exercise. Simply press the tips of the fingers of one hand against the same fingers of the other hand, and press until the palms come together. Get into the habit of doing this for twenty presses before and after each meal. Of course, the meals have nothing to do with it, but it sets up a routine and this is most important for exercising. Gary Player believes in press-ups, and I understand he does forty when he gets up in the morning and another forty before he turns in at night.

Archie Compston had a good trick for strengthening hands and fingers. He used to hold a driver with one hand (alternately) at the end of the shaft and with it pointing upwards, he used to go through the motions of writing his name on the ceiling!

Work out your own hand and forearm exercises to suit the life you lead. If you work in an office and play only at weekends, you must do more exercises than if your job entails manual labour. Get into the habit of doing one-, two-, three-finger drills as you go to get your bus—and don't bother about what folk think.

I am not sure that I fully agree with the use of a weighted golf club for exercise swinging. Sometimes this gives a hooking tendency when you start to use your normal lighter driver on the course. On the other hand, some golfers swear by them. So players must choose their own ways to produce hand and wrist muscles.

So many things about golf depend on personal preference. I am the happy possessor of good, fairly big, strong hands, yet I like the grips of my clubs to be thinner than usual. I have never been happy with thick grips, but I would not attempt to influence a beginner in this matter.

Next to milking a cow, the best hand, wrist and forearm exercise I know is wood-chopping. Use a long-handled weighty axe and don't be afraid to use plenty of wrist-cock when you reach the back of the swing. As a matter of fact, the actual swing that a woodman adopts to cut down a tree is very much the same as a full-pivot drive. Like the golfer, he must achieve great speed at impact. And that brings us to timing.

I would go so far as to say that the only 'timing drill' you can do in the garden is wood-chopping. The swinging movement is first-class for cultivating 'feel'. It helps the swinger to become 'weight conscious' so that he can make the speed accelerate to the maximum at the bottom of the arc.

Few people actually enjoy this kind of physical culture. However, it is necessary. Console yourself that you can add yards to your drive by dedication to regular exercise.

22

PREPARATION FOR THE 19TH HOLE

DARE I hope that you have read my book so far, and that you have assimilated the hints? If so, I am quite sure you have reached the proficiency to get plenty of fun from the game. Assuming this, it is right that you should know about this great colourful world which you have just entered. It will assist in your dedication; help you to become an addict.

Enthusiasts must be familiar with their subject; in golf, this means knowing about the great characters, amateur and professional, who have played an important part in the evolution of our game.

As a tournament player, closely involved in the competitive side of golf, perhaps I may be forgiven for writing these historical notes around the Open Championship.

The first Championship was played in 1860, when golf really got under way as a popular sport. The game had been played and enjoyed for years; in fact early records show that it was played as far back as in 1457. But until the mid-nineteenth century, it was an expensive pastime. The balls were made of feathers, tightly packed into small leather cases, and at half-a-crown each, they were far too costly for the ordinary man. In 1848, the 'feathery' was replaced by a much cheaper (and better) ball made of gutta-percha, and called the 'gutty'. They were mass-produced, cost very little, and made the game possible for a large, fascinated public.

Twelve years later, the Prestwick Golf Club offered a prize

The 19th HOLE

called the Champion Belt. It was to be competed for annually over the Prestwick twelve-hole course. Each championship was to be determined over thirty-six holes—three times round the circuit. The Belt, valued at £30, was to become the absolute property of any golfer, amateur or professional, who won the event three years running. Prize-money totalled £5.

Willie Park was the first Champion with a score of 174.

This was the hey-day of the Tom Morrises—perhaps the greatest father and son combination the game has ever known. Old Tom Morris won the Belt four times, but not consecutively. It was his son who carried off the trophy for keeps—winning in 1868, '69 and '70.

Each year the tournament attracted more golfers, and a growing public took a serious interest in the game.

In 1872 the Belt was replaced by a Cup, joint gift from St. Andrews, Prestwick and Musselburgh, and over these courses the Championship was played in annual rotation for the next twenty years. The names of the great players in those days are blazoned across colourful golfing history: Wee Jamie Anderson, who won the Cup three times and also claimed distinction by being the first competitor to hole in one; Tom Kidd, a caddie at St. Andrews, who won with the extraordinary score of 179; Jack Burns, a plasterer's mate, whose victory in '88 secured for him a job as greenkeeper at Warwick; David Brown, a slater by trade, who was known throughout Scotland for his big-hitting; John Ball, who was not only the first amateur to win but also the first Englishman, after a Scottish monopoly of thirty years; Hugh Kirkaldy, who caused a sensation with a nine-hole score of 33 at St. Andrews in 1891.

1892 was important. The Open Championship was extended to 72 holes, an entry fee was imposed for the first time, and Scotland's domination was over.

Three men burst on to the sporting scene and became internationally famous. Between 1892 and the outbreak of the First World War—twenty-two years—these great players had won the Open Championship no fewer than sixteen times. The 'Triumvirate' had arrived—Harry Vardon, J. H. Taylor and James Braid.

In 1900 Britain was at war with South Africa, the motor-car had arrived, and J. H. Taylor won his third title with a score of 309 over the Old Course at St. Andrews. By this time, Vardon too, had scored three wins, and Braid, never far down the list, was about to add his name to the list of winners for the first time.

In 1902, the 'gutty' was superseded by the rubber-cored ball, and gradually our modern ball evolved. Many senior golfers who remember playing the 'gutty' claim that it gave the game a tremendous challenge. But as the rubber-cored ball made the game easier, it opened up golf to thousands more people. Leading newspapers of the day began to report the Open Championship, and Vardon, Taylor and Braid became household names, even to non-golfers.

By now, the number of entrants for the Open exceeded a hundred. The prize-money had grown to £100, of which the winner received £30.

James Braid became a national hero when he chalked up five victories in the first decade of the twentieth century. In 1910 he became the first man to break 300 for four rounds in the Championship which he won at St. Andrews with 299—a feat equivalent in those days to Roger Bannister's sub-four-minute mile. The prize-money was raised again and Braid took home a cheque for £50.

As a golfer you must know these things. Part of the game is social and you will enjoy the talk at the 19th hole where matches past and present are replayed a hundred times.

On with our story. In 1913 J. H. Taylor scored his fifth triumph, at Hoylake, with a score of 304. Vardon followed with his sixth at Prestwick in 1914, then Britain went to war.

The Championship courses were deserted and the Record Books were locked away for five years.

In 1920, Lloyd George was Prime Minister, and George Duncan became the new British Champion at Deal. An American, Jim Barnes, played good golf and finished sixth. No one knew it then, but Barnes and his colleagues on the other side of the Atlantic were about to launch their indomitable attack on British golf.

Between 1921 and 1933 only one Briton held the title. That was Arthur Havers, who won at Troon in 1923.

The Roaring Twenties were highlighted by the successes of America's greatest golfers of the time—Hagen, and the amateur Bobby Jones.

Walter Hagen crammed his four Open victories into eight years. Jones won in '26, '27 and '30. In the latter year he swept the board on both sides of the Atlantic, winning the American and British Open and Amateur Championships. In 1927 he won at St. Andrews with a total of 285, the lowest score so far recorded. That year, a young man called Henry Cotton, professional at Langley Park, came ninth.

Tommy Armour, the American who learned his golf in Edinburgh, won the 1931 Open, and had a last round of 71 over the gruelling Carnoustie course. 1932 was Gene Sarazen's year. The great showman finished well ahead of the field at Sandwich. In 1933 American players filled five of the first six places. Winner was Desmond Shute. This was Britain's darkest hour, but on the distant horizon there flickered the dawn of a new era of British golf.

At Sandwich, in 1934, a young English colossus appeared and gave home golf the fillip it needed.

This was Henry Cotton's first victory, and it was probably the most sensational. After two rounds he was far ahead of the field with a score of 132. He retained the lead after the third. Then, with one round to go there was almost tragedy. Cotton had a stomach upset which nearly ruined his game. Nerves came in; he developed a hook, took 40 to the turn, but finished courageously in 79. That night he was a national hero.

Alf Perry had a runaway win at Muirfield, in 1935, and the enthusiasts felt that British golf was firmly on the map again. Meanwhile prize-money had risen to £500, of which the winner received £100.

Alf Padgham took the '36 title, and Cotton, R. A. Whitcombe and Dick Burton won the remaining pre-war Championships.

Then Hitler started his game.

Golf courses were ploughed up and clubhouses were used as
  G.—8

Land-Girl dormitories. Professionals and members alike locked away their golf bags and joined the Services.

The golfing world (by then there were about 750,000 golfers in Britain) had a happy reunion in 1946 at St. Andrews. To celebrate the return of the Open, the prize-money shot up to £1000. Sam Snead, the American, headed the field of 225, and a young South African, Bobby Locke, finished second. Dai Rees, like the rest of us just out of uniform, had a third round of 67 and was well up the list.

1947 was Irishman Fred Daly's year; in '48 Cotton won his third.

1949 was the year of the dramatic ball-in-the-bottle incident which can be said to have robbed Harry Bradshaw of victory. Bradshaw, playing grand golf, found his ball had rolled into a broken bottle during his second round at Sandwich. He played the shot with his blaster and risked the danger of flying glass. He took seven strokes at the hole, and it was some time before he recovered composure. Finally he tied with Bobby Locke on 283, but the South African won the play-off.

The Festival of Britain, the Coronation of Queen Elizabeth, the Conquest of Everest, and the arrival of a determined group of Commonwealth professionals, were some of the hall-marks of the Fifties. Locke, Thomson and Player dominated the British Open Championship. Locke won his second in 1950, his third in '52, and his fourth in '57. Peter Thomson became the first man to win three times consecutively—in '54, '55, '56—since Bob Ferguson in 1882. He won again in '58. Gary Player, the game little South African, took the title in 1959.

Two men prevented the Commonwealth players from making a clean sweep of the Fifties. Yours truly took the trophy in 1951, and Ben Hogan added the British Open to his long list of golfing honours in '53 at Carnoustie.

A centenary of anything is worth mentioning, but when it applies to the British Open Golf Championship it is something indeed. As was proper, this great gathering took place at St. Andrews in 1960, and it was attended by the most distinguished field of players and spectators who had ever gathered for any golf tournament. Indeed, it may never be repeated. A dozen past British Champions actually competed, and at the dinner given to us by the town of St. Andrews there were many more present.

On the last day of the Championship there fell a deluge of rain, the like of which had never before been seen at St. Andrews. At one time, the home green was a deep lake!

For the postponed last round there was a tremendous battle between Arnold Palmer, from the U.S.A., and Kel Nagle of Australia. Nagle won with a splendid four-round score of 278, one stroke better than ever before for a St. Andrews Championship. Nagle was a popular winner and I suppose for a Commonwealth player to succeed was next best thing to a home player.

Arnold Palmer, who now must be a millionaire in dollars, son of a chief-greenkeeper, won the Championships of 1961, at Birkdale and 1962, at Troon.

In 1963, history was again made. The title, for the first time, was won by a left-handed golfer. Bob Charles, from New Zealand, proved something we all know: the man who can putt really well always wins.

A new name was engraved on the silver ewer in 1964. It was Tony Lema, a colourful American with a watertight golf style and tremendous 'crowd appeal'.

So, there you have the story of the British Open Championship, still the most coveted prize in golf.

It would be too much to hope that any intending golfer who progresses as a result of this book will be a British Champion (although less likely things have happened). Nevertheless, an even greater reward may well be within reach.

I said it in the opening chapter and I repeat it again: if you are instructed and stimulated into dedication for this great game, you will surely be a happy man. Assuming good health and a fair livelihood, golf gives the richest fun life has to offer.

SLOPING LIES

● WHEN STANDING ABOVE, THE BALL WILL GO RIGHT, SO AIM WELL TO THE LEFT OF TARGET.

● STAND CLOSE TO THE BALL WITH WEIGHT BACK ON THE HEELS.

THIS IS A 'HANGING' LIE

● WHEN STANDING BELOW, MOST OF YOUR WEIGHT SHOULD BE ON THE LEFT FOOT.

● PLAY THE BALL OFF THE LEFT FOOT, BUT DON'T 'QUIT' OR YOU WILL STAB THE GROUND.

● AIM TO THE RIGHT.

- ● FIRST, RELAX WITH PRACTICE SWINGS
  - THE CLUBHEAD MUST CUT THROUGH THE GRASS WITHOUT 'STRAIN-RESTRICTION'

- ● ADDRESS THE BALL WITH A SLIGHTLY OPEN CLUBFACE

- ● DON'T ATTEMPT DISTANCE — CONCENTRATE ON SWINGING THROUGH TO GET OUT.

— The JUNGLE SHOT —

GOLFING DICTIONARY

As a subject for conversation, golf is endless. George Houghton, who did the illustrations in this book, calls golf-talk the 'emotional traffic' of the game.

Like doctors and scientists, we golfers have a language of our own. Here is a glossary of terms and phrases, ancient and modern, which will be useful.

Air-Shot	A stroke played at the ball, which misses completely. Air-shots must be counted and are included in the score.
Albatross	A score of three shots under bogey for any particular hole; e.g. completing a bogey five in two shots. Chances against are tens of thousands to one.
'All Square'	Means 'level'. At the end, it means the match is a draw.
'As We Lie'	Phrase used by a player indicating that he has taken the same number of strokes on a particular hole as his opponent.
Ball	English size: 1·62 inches in diameter. American size: 1·68 inches. Having less wind-resistance the English ball goes a little further from the tee, but does not 'sit up' so well on the fairway. Many golfers prefer the American ball for

chipping and putting. Current American domination of the game suggests the larger ball gets better results. Give it a try.

Birdie   One shot better than bogey for the hole.

Blind Shot   A shot played at an out-of-sight target.

Bogey   Currently being replaced by 'Par'. For a hole, it is the number of shots which a first-class player is expected to take in ideal weather conditions. The bogey, or par, for a course is the sum total of the bogeys on each hole.

Brassie   A two-wood, before clubs had numbers.

Caddie   Professional club-carrier. Good ones are experts on the game and worth their weight in gold. Fees: from ten shillings to £1 a round. Fast dying race since the coming of caddie-carts, the mechanical contraption on two wheels on which the golf bag is carried.

Cleek   Club used at the beginning of the century; a shallow-faced one-iron.

Curtis Cup   Played for by teams of ladies representing Britain and the United States. Takes place on alternate years.

Divot   Clod of earth usually removed when the ball is correctly hit with an iron club. Must be replaced!

Dog-Leg   Describes a hole where a ball cannot be hit from tee to green in a straight line.

Driving-   Comparatively new in this country, but rapidly
Range   becoming as popular as they have been since 1948 in the United States. Up to sixty golfers can practise down a common fairway, hiring golf balls by the bucket at a penny-a-shot. Some ranges are floodlit for use by night. Advantages: an inexhaustible supply of golf

balls, and someone else has the job of picking them up.

Eagle A score of two shots under the bogey for a hole.

Fairway The regularly cut stretch of smooth grass between tee and green.

Fore! Golfers' cry of warning. When you hear it, duck immediately; someone behind has rudely hit a ball which is coming perilously close.

Fourball A two-a-side game in which each golfer plays with his own ball, and the best counts for the side.

Foursome A two-a-side game in which each side plays with one ball, which is struck alternately by both players. Drives are taken in turn, no matter who played the last shot on the previous hole.

Green The putting surface. Also, the old name for a golf course—still referred to this way in Scotland.

Handicap The system of 'evening up' the game. Reflects a player's current form, and enables him to play against any opponent on equal terms.

Hole-in-One To hole out with a tee-shot. The feat permits you to wear a special tie, and appoints you host for drinks all round.

Hook Shot which sends the ball sharply from right to left. Usually caused by holding the club with the right hand too far under the shaft, or showing too many knuckles of the left hand.

L.G.U. Ladies' Golf Union—looks after the golfing interests of the fair sex.

Links Seaside golf courses. Inland, they are just 'courses'.

Loft	Angle of the club-face in relation to the shaft.
Mashie	Old term for what we now call a five-iron.
Match-Play	The term for a game which is decided by the number of holes won and lost. A match is over when a player is 'up' by more holes than the number which remain to be played, e.g. four up and three to play. In competitive golf, where the score is still level after eighteen holes, the match is continued until one player wins a hole. In friendly games, extra holes are not usually played. A draw is 'all square'.
Medal-Play	Means 'stroke' play, in which the score for the complete round is recorded. In the past, tournaments were 'match-play' with the rare exception of when a Royal and Ancient Medal was competed for. Now, stroke-play is common enough and is still referred to as 'Medal' play.
Niblick	Old term meaning a seven- or eight-iron, depending on requirements. A mashie-niblick was like a six-iron.
P.G.A.	Professional Golfers' Association. Governing body of British professionals.
Par	See 'Bogey'.
Pivot	The 'turn' of the upper and middle part of the body when winding up for a golf swing.
Rough	Uncut areas of the course, which provide natural hazard.
Rub of the Green	Occurs when a ball in motion is stopped or deflected by an 'outside agency'.
Ryder Cup	Played for on alternate years between British and American professionals.
S.S.S.	Standard Scratch Score. Basic score on which

handicaps are assessed, determined by length of course and difficulty of terrain.

Scratch Golfer   Player who goes round his home course consistently in the Standard Scratch Score, and has a handicap of 0.

Shank   Most heartbreaking shot in golf, when the ball is struck with that part of the club where the shaft joins the clubhead (the 'neck'). Also known as the 'socket'. Usually caused by 'rolling' the wrists and swinging from 'out to in'.

'Sixes'   A game which can be played by three players, all against all. Players compete for six points a hole—winner takes 4, second 2. If two players tie they take 3 each; if all tie they each take 2.

Slice   Most common fault in golf. Caused by hitting the ball from 'out to in'. The ball swings sharply from left to right, hits the ground, kicks right and refuses to roll.

Spoon   Old term, what we now call a three-wood.

Stableford   A popular form of competition, worked on a points basis. Scoring: 1 point for a hole played in one-over bogey, 2 points for a bogey, 3 for a birdie, etc.

Stroke Allowance   Number of strokes given or received when playing on handicap. In singles (match-play) take $\frac{3}{4}$ of the difference in handicaps; in foursomes take $\frac{3}{8}$ of the difference of the combined handicaps. For Stableford, the allowance is $\frac{7}{8}$ of handicap.

Stymie   No longer in use, but worth knowing for historical interest. A stymie was achieved on the green by hitting your ball so that it stopped on the line directly between the hole and your opponent's ball. Usually an accidental hazard which, by many, was considered an element of luck giving unfair advantage.

Tee
Small plastic or wooden peg on which to 'tee up' the ball for driving. Also, the 'teeing ground' from which the drive is played.

Topped Shot
When the club-face hits the ball above the 'equator line' and sends it running along the ground instead of in the air. Normal cause: raising the head too quickly, which imperceptibly raises the left shoulder—and the club.

Walker Cup
Played for on alternate years between teams of Amateurs representing Britain and the United States.

DON'TS to REMEMBER

1. THE 'PICCOLO' GRIP WITH A LOOSE LEFT

2. OVERSWING — DESTROYS BALANCE

3. INSUFFICIENT TURN

4. RIGHT LEG TOO STIFF

5. KNEE POINTS OUT — INSTEAD OF RIGHT

6. THE BALL SHOULD BE OPPOSITE LEFT HEEL AT ADDRESS.

THIS SHOT WILL SURELY BE AN OUT TO IN HORROR

7. ELBOWS HAVE BROKEN TOO SOON
8. HEAD-UP
9. HIPS HAVEN'T TURNED
10. WEIGHT SHOULD HAVE TRANSFERRED TO LEFT

TWO CLASSIC ← EXAMPLES → OF THE SLICE